How Would JESUS

VOTE?

**A Christian Perspective
on the Issues**

D. James Kennedy, PhD
and Jerry Newcombe

WATERBROOK
PRESS

HOW WOULD JESUS VOTE?
PUBLISHED BY WATERBROOK PRESS
12265 Oracle Boulevard, Suite 200
Colorado Springs, Colorado 80921
A division of Random House Inc.

All Scripture quotations, unless otherwise indicated, are taken from the New King James Version®. Copyright © 1982 by Thomas Nelson Inc. Used by permission. All rights reserved. Scripture quotations marked (ESV) are taken from The Holy Bible, English Standard Version, copyright © 2001 by Crossway Bibles, a division of Good News Publishers. Used by permission. All rights reserved. Scripture quotations marked (KJV) are taken from the King James Version. Scripture quotations marked (NIV) are taken from the Holy Bible, New International Version®. NIV®. Copyright © 1973, 1978, 1984 by International Bible Society. Used by permission of Zondervan Publishing House. All rights reserved.

Italics in Scripture quotations reflect the author's added emphasis.

ISBN 978-1-4000-7406-8

Library of Congress Cataloging-in-Publication Data
Kennedy, D. James (Dennis James), 1930-
    How would Jesus vote? : a Christian perspective on the issues / D. James Kennedy & Jerry Newcombe. — 1st ed.
        p. cm.
    Includes bibliographical references (p.).
    ISBN 978-1-4000-7406-8
    1. Christianity and politics—United States. 2. Church and social problems—United States. I. Newcombe, Jerry. II. Title.
    BR526.K465 2008
    261.70973—dc22
                        2007029984

Printed in the United States of America
2008

10 9 8 7 6 5 4 3

Special Sales
Most WaterBrook Multnomah books are available in special quantity discounts when purchased in bulk by corporations, organizations, and special interest groups. Custom imprinting or excerpting can also be done to fit special needs. For information, please e-mail SpecialMarkets@WaterBrookPress.com or call 1-800-603-7051.

To Bill Jensen,

our book agent, who has done such a wonderful job

Contents

PART III: FINAL THOUGHTS

Foreword

Secular forces are not planning on withdrawing from politics. They don't believe in divorcing their worldview from their policy advocacy, their governance, or their law making. But they seem to want Christians to withdraw.

Sadly, too many Christians have bought into the lie that the letter or spirit of the First Amendment precludes their participation or involvement in the political arena. How can responsible Christians even consider unilateral surrender? And why are they always asked to make the false choice between their politics and their evangelism? They can and should do both, with vigor.

There is, after all, a partial interdependency between politics and religion. In the absence of political freedom, the Christian's ability to evangelize and honor the Great Commission is severely diminished. Similarly, public policy both reflects and affects our society's values. If Christians opt out, they can expect laws that are less representative of or wholly hostile to their values—sometimes with life-or-death consequences.

By refusing to "get their hands dirty" in the material world of politics, or discouraging other Christians from doing so, they might, unwittingly, be aiding and abetting the transformation of our culture and society away from Christian values, irrespective of whether they are otherwise doing their part at evangelizing and serving as exemplary witnesses for Christ. Indeed, if our largely Christian Founding Fathers had subscribed to the modern view that Christians should keep their values privatized and segregated from the policies they advocate, this nation, as a nonpareil bastion of freedom, would never have been established.

Newsweek's Anna Quindlen recently wrote that a presidential victory for Rudy Giuliani "wouldn't be a good thing for this country, but his candidacy may wind up being a very good thing for his party," which Quindlen obviously believes has been hijacked by the Christian Right. Giuliani's strong poll numbers, said Quindlen, perhaps "indicate that the end is nigh for the stranglehold the Leviticus lobby has had on the GOP."[1]

It's no longer surprising that those screaming most loudly against Christianity and its influence on public policy in America often employ the same tactics and represent the same dangers they falsely attribute to Christians. Christians have far more to fear from the secular thought police than the other way around.

Whether it's writer Christopher Hitchens or CNN's Christiane Amanpour sloppily conflating Christian "fundamentalists" or observant Jews with Islamic jihadists, secular leftists calling the Christian Right the American Taliban, or militant secularists like HBO's Bill Maher salivating over reports that Mother Teresa had a crisis of faith, the theme is the same: Christian activists are a societal nuisance.

The secularists seek to remove God from the Pledge of Allegiance, though one poll reveals that only 14 percent of Americans agree with them.

They brand as bigots opponents of the societal sanctioning of homosexual marriage. Some even pronounce certain scriptural passages on homosexuality "hate speech" that leads to violence, as if to disapprove of any behavior is to hate it or its practitioners and leads to violence against them. This same theme is behind proposed congressional "hate crime" legislation that would criminalize the enunciation of certain scriptures.

Likewise, many pro-abortionists speciously argue that pro-life advocacy leads to violence against women—never mind the violence against the unborn.

The secular left condemns traditionalists for "legislating morality" and invading our bedrooms. Their quasi-religious fervor apparently blinds them to their efforts to wield governmental power to impose their own values, whether on homosexual marriage, abortion, wealth redistribution, or socialized medicine.

Secularists have every right to advocate the adoption of their values by our society. But they are hypocritical to deny they do so and to castigate Christians for doing the same.

Because I believe Christians have a duty to be involved in the political process, or at least not discourage those who choose such involvement, I am pleased to recommend this new book by the late Dr. D. James Kennedy and Jerry Newcombe. It presents a compelling case—demonstrating that duty—and explains why Christians should, unapologetically, apply Christian values to their policy advocacy and their vote.

David Limbaugh
Nationally syndicated columnist and
author of the *NYT* bestsellers *Absolute
Power, Persecution,* and *Bankrupt*
October 2007

Acknowledgments

There are so many to thank...and so little time, but let us try.

First of all, we are both grateful to our wives for all their help and their patience as we labored on the book. So thank you, Anne and Kirsti, who also edited different versions of the manuscript.

Also, I must thank my ever-efficient secretary, Mary Anne Bunker, for everything. Also we thank Nancy Britt for her help with the editing.

We are also grateful to our literary agent, Bill Jensen, for doing so much to get the message of this book out to a much wider audience. He is doing an excellent job, and this book is dedicated to him.

We are thankful to John Rabe in the television department of Coral Ridge Ministries, who provided helpful research for this book. John has an excellent knack for looking up sources and ferreting out fact from fiction. John even helped with writing a portion of the judicial activism chapter.

Finally, we are grateful to Brian Fisher, head of Coral Ridge Ministries. He has led the ministry so capably during very trying times, always striving to apply God's principles in all things.

Part I

JESUS AND POLITICS

Do Jesus and Politics Mix?

But Peter and John replied,
"Judge for yourselves whether it is right
in God's sight to obey you
rather than God."

—Acts 4:19, NIV

Jesus and politics. They do not mix. Or so we have been told.

Jesus is certainly above politics. The question is, would He have His followers be involved in the political process? On the one hand, we should not put our trust in princes. Syndicated columnist Cal Thomas likes to point out that salvation will not come on Air Force One. Fair enough. Erwin Lutzer, an author and pastor, reminds us that the Cross can accomplish things politics cannot. I agree completely and invest most of my time in evangelism and discipleship. On the other hand, I also believe we must be involved in the political process.

There's no question conservative Christianity is important in politics. In the wake of the 2006 elections, some "progressive" leaders among the Republicans blamed the religious Right for Democrat gains. Dr. James Dobson of Focus on the Family shot back: "Values voters are not going to carry the water for the Republican Party if it ignores their deeply held convictions and beliefs."[1] Dobson warned the Republican leadership to think twice before it abandoned "their pro-moral, pro-family and pro-life base."[2] Meanwhile, a November 2006 poll shows that fewer Christians trust the GOP as faith-friendly: "The number of people who consider the GOP friendly to religion dropped from 55 percent to 47 percent."[3] In November 2006, *Newsweek* magazine devoted a cover story to "The Politics of Jesus,"[4] while a February 2007 editorial in *Time* magazine shouted "The Religious Right's Era Is Over."[5] The same month, Christian Newswire declared that evangelicals are the nation's single largest voting bloc.[6] Even Hillary Clinton, who in 2001 said, "I wonder if it's possible to be a Republican and a Christian at the same time,"[7] recently hired an evangelical consultant to build bridges between her and the faith community.[8]

Any way you look at it, Jesus and politics are a hot topic.

FEAR OF THE RELIGIOUS RIGHT

A former writer for the *New York Times,* Christopher Hedges, wrote a book titled *American Fascists: The Christian Right and the War on America.* In a recent commentary about the book, Don Feder, an orthodox Jew, said,

> Hedges' screed is the latest in a long, long, line of hysterical tracts denouncing what the secular left calls the Religious Right. The past year alone has seen such saliva-specked exposés of alleged Christian extremism as:
>
> ★ *Religion Gone Bad: Hidden Dangers of the Christian Right* by Mel White
> ★ *Why the Christian Right Is Wrong* by Robin Meyers
> ★ *The Left Hand of God: Taking Back Our Country from the Religious Right* by Michael Lerner
> ★ *Theocons: Secular America Under Siege* by Damon Linker
> ★ *American Theocracy* by Kevin Phillips
> ★ *The Baptizing of America: The Religious Right's Plan for the Rest of Us* by James Rudin
> ★ *Piety and Politics: The Right Wing Assault on Religious Freedom* by the Reverend Barry Lynn and

★ *Kingdom Coming: The Rise of Christian Nationalism* by Michelle Goldberg.

The objective of all of this Chicken Little squawking is to convince us that the Constitution is falling—that conservative Christians intend to abolish the Bill of Rights, outlaw sin and replace democracy with a theocratic state that will make Calvin's Geneva look like Hugh Hefner's bachelor party....

Hedges quotes evangelist [D. James] Kennedy: "As vice regents of God, we are to exercise godly dominion and influence over our neighborhoods, our schools, our government" and "our entertainment media, our news media, our scientific endeavors...."

How successful the religious right has been in exercising "godly dominion" over the news media and Hollywood may be seen by picking up the *New York Times,* tuning in to *CNN* or *NPR* or experiencing the torrent of sex and violence (not to mention the ubiquitous attacks on Christianity) in movies shown every evening on cable television.

Kennedy and his colleagues are saying that Christians have a right and a duty to bring their values into the political arena. Shocking![9]

So here we are in an interesting place. Many in this country, it seems, would prefer that evangelical Christians remain absent from the political process. And yet, for the last decade or so, many Christians, including myself, have taken an active stand in politics, giving the other side plenty to be upset about.

Are Christians really to blame for the problems facing our nation today? Perhaps an analogy might help.

THE CASE OF DR. FRANKENSTEIN'S MONSTER

We all are aware of the alarming statistics being generated across our nation.

★ epidemic crime

★ plummeting educational achievement

★ pornography infiltrating our homes, even those of some pastors

★ the breakdown of the family

★ widespread acceptance of immorality

Clearly, our society is in a great need of a true awakening. I believe it is our only real hope.

What happened along the way from Plymouth Rock to the present? Who is responsible? Was it the atheists? the humanists? the secularists? the communists? the cultists? the New Agers? the hedonists? the ACLU? NOW? the People for the American Way?

Let me tell you a story. You remember it, I am sure. Just imagine, if you will, that final scene in Mary Shelley's *Frankenstein* when the monster has gone berserk and has wreaked havoc upon the townspeople. He's left scores of people dead, and now he's coming after his maker. He's destroyed his home, and the whole thing is now ablaze and setting the sky alight.

Imagine that, just then, a friend of Frankenstein arrives from a distant city and sees the carnage and the chaos and asks, "Dr. Frankenstein, what has happened here?"

"A monster, a monster!" says the doctor.

The friend is confused. "What are you talking about?"

"A monster did this. It was terrible! He went berserk, killing people and destroying my home!"

"A monster? Where in the world did it come from?"

Silence.

"Dr. Frankenstein? Where did the monster come from?"

The doctor's face falls. "I...I created it. I made it myself."

In case you do not see the application, my friend, we have to acknowledge that a great deal of the blame for the state of the nation must fall upon *us*. It must be placed at the doorstep of the church. We have failed to obey the Great Commission in this country. We have failed to obey our cultural mandate to be involved in every sphere of social activity. We have retreated from politics, from social involvement, from the media, and from higher education. Now chaos has broken loose, and we look at the scene before us with horror.

We may not have created this monster with our own hands, but we have allowed it to grow and take power. With the power of the government, the colleges, the courts, the legislatures, and the media, it has wreaked this disaster—this carnage in America today. Christians have failed to fulfill their responsibilities as citizens in this country, and we have allowed this great blessing of a godly nation to slip through our hands.

WHAT PARTY DOES GOD CLAIM?

What side is God on? People have wanted to know that since the beginning of warfare. During the Civil War, people wondered which side God was on. Initially many pastors and their congregations were duped by Adolf Hitler. Journalist and historian William L. Shirer, author of *The Rise and Fall of the Third Reich*, notes that some German "Christians" even drew up a resolution (which ultimately was not adopted) demanding "One People, One Reich, One Faith," and these same professing believers wanted to require "all pastors to take an oath of allegiance to Hitler."[10] Surely, God did not approve of Hitler's anti-Jewish, anti-Christian, antifreedom regime.

In the book of Joshua, the title character has an encounter with God, or more precisely, the Son of God:

Now when Joshua was near Jericho, he looked up and saw a man standing in front of him with a drawn sword in his hand. Joshua went up to him and asked, "Are you for us or for our enemies?"

"Neither," he replied, "but as commander of the army of the LORD I have now come." Then Joshua fell facedown to the ground in reverence, and asked him, "What message does my Lord have for his servant?" (Joshua 5:13–14, NIV)

Interpreting this passage, we know it was Jesus because of the parallel in Revelation 1. Line up the two passages, and you find even some of the same phrases applied to the divine man with the sword who appeared in both cases (further, whenever men attempted to worship an angel, the angel would rebuke them). Joshua asks Jesus, "Are you on our side?" much the same way we ask today, "Lord, are you on our side or theirs?"

And how does Jesus answer? "Neither." In some versions the word is translated "No." He is not on anybody's side. Jesus said that He was the commander—Joshua's captain and the Lord of the battle. He commands not only His people but the days of all people and the host of heaven as well.

We want to vote "correctly," but how do we know the right way to vote—the Christian way to vote? Throughout history, many people have been burned by thinking their party was right. There was even a so-called Christian party in Nazi Germany when virtually the whole country jumped on the bandwagon. These professing Christians dared to align the name of Jesus Christ with Adolf Hitler's diabolical goals.

Jesus goes on to explain to Joshua that he will be victorious if he obeys the Lord and does what he is commanded to do. The question, therefore, is not if God is on our side, but rather, *are we on God's side?*

You may recall that Abraham Lincoln said as much during the Civil War. In 1863 he overheard someone say that he hoped "the Lord was on the Union's side." The president responded: "I know that the Lord is always on the side of the right. But it is my constant anxiety and prayer that I and this nation should be on the Lord's side."[11]

Does God care how we cast our ballot? I believe the answer is yes. For many years Christians have abstained from politics, and now they are shocked that the culture around them has deteriorated. Certainly, we should not rely solely on political power to right the world's wrongs. All politicians are human. Even the best of them will disappoint. Yet how would Jesus have us vote? When Jesus was on earth, He did not reside in a democratic republic and had no opportunity to cast a ballot. Meanwhile, those of us who make following Him our first priority believe He has spoken through His Word and given us principles that can inform us on how to vote on many issues.

The purpose of this book is to explore those biblical principles from which we can draw political implications. Does the Bible say anything about how we are to educate our young? Does it say anything about abortion or capital punishment? Does it say anything about war or how we are to vote on the environment, immigration, or health care? Sincere Christians may have different views on how to tackle these issues. However, I trust that we have grace enough to respect Christians on either side of the partisan aisle.

In this book, we will begin by looking at the broader question of whether the Bible and politics can—and should—mix. I believe that they do. Jesus said we are to "render therefore to Caesar the things that are Caesar's, and to God the things that are God's" (Luke 20:25). Furthermore, we are called to be salt and light, which has political implications. After exploring the Bible and politics, we will examine the critical issues of our nation and look for guidance from the Bible. This discussion will include many of the issues currently tearing us apart as a society.

Some may quibble that we should look only at what Jesus said as opposed to the whole Bible. Yet Jesus put His seal of approval on the Old Testament as the Word of God, saying, for example, "The Scripture cannot be broken" (John 10:35) and "Do not think that I came to destroy the Law or the Prophets. I did not come to destroy but to fulfill. For assuredly, I say to you, till heaven and earth pass away, one jot or one tittle will by no means pass from the law till all is fulfilled" (Matthew 5:17–18). Not one jot or tittle—much less a word, a sentence, or an entire prophetic book—should be ignored. He said that if people would not believe Moses and the prophets (that is, the Old Testament), then they wouldn't believe if someone (that is, Himself) came back from the dead (see Luke 16:31).

Jesus commissioned the writing of the New Testament to record His words and the further revelation He would give through the Holy Spirit. In John 16, Jesus told those He sent (the apostles):

I still have many things to say to you, but you cannot bear them now. However, when He, the Spirit of truth, has come, He will guide you into all truth; for He will not speak on His own authority, but whatever He hears He will speak; and He will tell you things to come. He will glorify Me, for He will take of what is Mine and declare it to you. All things that the Father has are Mine. Therefore I said that He will take of Mine and declare it to you. (John 16:12–15)

It was by His authority that the apostles wrote His words and further revelation. Nothing was accepted in the New Testament except that which

11

clearly had apostolic authority.[12] The whole Bible, not just the words of Jesus, was given *by God:* "All Scripture is given by inspiration of God, and is profitable for doctrine, for reproof, for correction, for instruction in righteousness, that the man of God may be complete, thoroughly equipped for every good work" (2 Timothy 3:16–17). When we ask, "How would Jesus have us vote?" we are actually asking, "How would the Bible have us vote?"

There are certainly some people in our time who make Jesus out to be something He was not and who convert Him into many things. Though He clearly taught against any violation of God's law, many people prefer to make Jesus into their own image without a shred of evidence. John Calvin once observed that the human heart is a factory of idols. The triune God detests all idolatry. The Jesus of the Bible is the Jesus with whom we have to deal, like it or not.

So let us humbly search the Scriptures to see if God has something to say on the political issues that are tearing apart our nation. Let us do so with the great motto sometimes attributed to Augustine, other times to Blaise Pascal: "In essentials, unity. In nonessentials, liberty. And in all things, charity."

"JESUS IS A LIBERAL"

Recently I saw a bumper sticker that said "Jesus is a liberal." This reminds me of a liberal seminarian who told one of my church members, "God is a conservative, but Jesus is a liberal." When the seminarian was challenged, he stammered a lot. He forgot that "Jesus" is the Greek form of the Hebrew name "Joshua," and Joshua was the Old Testament conquering hero whom God raised up to clear the land of the Canaanite people because their sin was so great that they had reached a point of no return. As Joshua was a liberator, so Jesus is the true liberator who saves those who trust in Him from their sins (including Joshua, who was looking forward to Him). In short, contrary to our seminary friend, there is continuity from the Old through the New Testament. Jesus did not come to abolish the law but to fulfill it.

Despite people's remakings of Him, Jesus was Semitic. He was a first-century Jew. He was not white, not black, not communist, not homosexual —not feminist, as one of Dan Brown's characters says in *The Da Vinci Code.*[13] Certainly, Jesus cared about women, but He was not a feminist the way many would define feminism today.

We have to deal with Jesus as He *is,* as we find Him in Scripture, not as we want Him to be.

CONSERVATIVE VS. LIBERAL

What is a conservative? What is a liberal? Are we talking about those who only want the status quo as opposed to those who desire liberty through new ways of thinking?

One man expressed it this way: "A conservative believes you are best qualified to take care of you and your family. A liberal believes the government is best qualified to take care of you and your family."

Someone else said that if you want to make a conservative, it is easy: just give him something to conserve.

I think we need to go beyond labels. To me, more important than being a conservative or a liberal is being a committed Christian. When I vote, do I please Jesus with my vote? One example comes to mind: how could He be pleased if I vote in a way that promotes the destruction of innocent human life? If a politician does not get the issues of life and death right, how is he going to get the other things right? It is sort of like a Christian theologian who does not have a correct view of the Trinity. If that is messed up, chances are good he will also get other areas of theology incorrect.

ARE WE LOSING GROUND?

Several years ago I had lunch with a missionary who had been in South America for a good many years. He said to me, in effect, "On my rare returns to the States, I see that there is an apparent evangelical awakening—a revival of sorts—superchurches, tremendous television and radio ministries, great crusades and conferences, and thousands of people coming out to them. How is it that I still see the whole moral fiber of the country continuing to slip? Why is there still the increasing pornography, the increasing ungodliness in the laws that are passed, and the unconcern for human life?"

The problem is that, though there are many Christians in this country, though we can say that about 36 percent of adults claim they have had a conversion experience,[14] and though that number is growing, it is still a minority. It just so happens that evangelical Christians are generally not making the laws in the Congress; they are not the ones running our television networks; they are not the ones printing pornographic material—or allowing the laws that permit it. Though Christianity may be growing in this country, it is still far from being the controlling force.

Have you ever wondered why even though so many Americans claim to be Christians, we seem to wield little influence in our culture? A recent study by LifeWay has found that many Christians and pastors are out of touch with the current culture.[15] We have much less political might than our numbers would suggest. Our beliefs and morals are often held up to ridicule and attacked in the media and on university and college campuses. You would think we were a small group of extremists, hanging on for dear life. This is hardly the image of "more than conquerors" that's often promoted in churches.

How often have you heard the assertion that politics and religion do not mix? Or "you can't legislate morality"? These kinds of statements are repeated so often that many people take them as gospel. Rev. Martin Luther King Jr. observed, "Even though morality cannot be legislated, behavior can be regulated. While the law cannot change the heart, it can certainly restrain the heartless."[16]

The very nature of legislation involves value judgments. Some things are deemed right and legal; other things are wrong and illegal. That is morality. I believe the question is not *if* morality can be legislated. The question is *whose* morality will be legislated?

In the political realm, we have been commanded by Christ to give Caesar what is Caesar's. Yet many Christians in America do not even bother to vote. In the area of the mainstream media, we seem to have very little influence.

How about the law? Imagine an evangelical judge being appointed to the U.S. Supreme Court. Say, for instance, Roy S. Moore, the so-called Ten Commandments Judge, was appointed. It would stir up such intense opposition that the character of such a judge would be besmirched from coast to coast. The hearings on Capitol Hill would make past hearings (like those that swirled around John Ashcroft when he was nominated for attorney general) seem like just another day in Washington.

Why are Christians so routinely maligned? Why are we so ineffective in legislating our morality? I believe we have traded the historic, traditional image of the sovereign Conqueror for a pale and meek buddy. We place our religion in our back pocket to take out when we need some comfort. Too many professing believers have a weak view of God, seeing Jesus as Lord of their individual lives and not as Lord of the nations. Christ may one day be enthroned as king over the whole earth, the One before whom each of us will stand, but this is far from us.

The Armenians have a beautiful phrase: "Christ, only Christ." These were the last words of thousands of Armenian Christians early in the twentieth century. During history's bloodiest century—an era when many nations tried to dethrone God and substitute a man-worshiping totalitarian state in His place—there were many massacres, the most notable being the Holocaust. One of the first massacres in the twentieth century was of hundreds of thousands of Armenian Christians at the hands of Muslim Turks. The estimates vary from six hundred thousand to over one million who were slaughtered. The Turks went through Christian villages in Armenia, lined up all the residents, and asked them one question: "Christ or Mohammed"? If the Christians chose Christ, they were bayoneted to death. Many of the Armenians not only chose Jesus, but they did so with the phrase "Christ, only Christ."

It is a good phrase, for He is the Sovereign One. He is the One with whom we all have to do. He is God's inescapable imperative. Would that more Christians recognized His sovereignty and the implications that Christ the King is enthroned on high.

JESUS IS NOT ON THE BALLOT

When Jesus Christ finished His earthly ministry, He ascended to heaven and was seated at the right hand of God the Father. I believe it was then His kingdom began (although, of course, it has not come in fullness). Colossians 1:13 tells us that we have been born into His kingdom, which, by implication, *has* begun (past tense). Hebrews 1:8 tells us that Jesus's throne is forever.

More than five hundred years before Jesus was born, Daniel said this about the coming Savior:

> I was watching in the night visions,
> And behold, One like the Son of Man,
> Coming with the clouds of heaven!

He came to the Ancient of Days,

And they brought Him near before Him.

Then to Him was given dominion and glory and a kingdom,

That all peoples, nations, and languages should serve Him.

His dominion is an everlasting dominion,

Which shall not pass away,

And His kingdom the one

Which shall not be destroyed. (Daniel 7:13–14)

No wonder King Herod tried to kill Jesus while He was just a baby. No wonder the Roman authorities, some thirty-three years later, crucified Him for the "crime" of being the "King of the Jews."

But Jesus is not on the ballot. The mistake in history (what we could call "the medieval mistake") is trying to impose His kingdom on others by force. To this day Islam is guilty of this error. Some professing Christians are guilty of this error today too (abortion-clinic bombers come to mind), but they are far and away the exception.

Since Jesus is not on the ballot, then no one who is perfect is on the ballot. That means we have to pick a sinner (or a list of sinners) whenever we cast a ballot. I suppose there are times when a Christian cannot in good conscience cast a ballot, but that is rare. What can we say for those Christians living in totalitarian regimes? On the other hand, we should have no excuse in a representative democracy like America.

Even though Jesus is the "Ruler of the nations," it is not up to Christians to try to bring in His kingdom by force. When people in times past attempted to usher in Christ's kingdom, they failed. No human being can usher in the millennium. Not Constantine. Not Pope Gregory the Great. Not Justinian. Not Charlemagne. Not John Calvin. Not John Winthrop.

Not Oliver Cromwell. Not Abraham Kuyper. Not Ronald Reagan. The kingdom of Christ will not be fully realized on planet Earth until God decides to convert and transform more and more enemies of Jesus. But that does not mean that between now and the time when Christ comes *in fullness* we can't experience at least partially the effects of His kingdom. "This universe is at war," observed C. S. Lewis. "It is a civil war, a rebellion, and... we are living in a part of the universe occupied by the rebel."[17] And herein lies the tension. We Christians, individually and corporately, can actually make a difference as to how much of our world is occupied by Christ versus how much is occupied by the devil.

We, the loyal subjects of Christ the King, can make a huge difference for good or evil in this world. We have the opportunity by our beliefs and actions to help shape the future for generations to come, until such a time as Christ once and for all ushers in His kingdom. We may be here for a short time or a long haul. In either event, it's unarguable—whatever your view of the end times—that we should be faithful in Christ's service until the time He returns (as alluded to in Luke 19:13).

When we consider how difficult are the times in which we live or how rampant evil seems to be, step back for a moment and reflect on how bad things once were. Christ was not born into a perfect world. In two thousand years the Christian faith has helped make vast changes in our world.[18] Theologian Lorraine Boettner observed, "Today we are living in an era that is relatively golden as compared with the first century of the Christian era. This progress is to go on until on this earth we shall see a practical fulfillment of the prayer, Thy kingdom come, Thy will be done in earth as it is in heaven."[19] For example, human beings are not slaughtered for sport as were the gladiators. The world at the time was *far* worse than it is today. Yet it's painfully obvious we have much further to go.

A THEOCRACY?

Modern secularists often accuse the religious Right of calling for a theocracy in America. Despite these claims, I am *not* advocating a theocracy. I am only trying to restore the truth that Christianity is, and always has been, a fundamental component in the marketplace of ideas.

Throughout history, there has been only one theocracy, and that was the state of Israel in the time of the Old Testament. God alone ruled then. There was no legislature. The Sanhedrin was simply a supreme court. There was but one lawgiver.

That system of law stopped with the destruction of Israel, ending the only theocracy in history. I would not have America reinstitute the Old Testament civil and legal systems to replace our governmental legislation.[20] Those laws are merely a guide to the kinds of laws that civil governments should form today. I do believe that the laws of every nation should be in harmony, not with the civil laws of the Old Testament, but at least with the moral laws of the Ten Commandments.

Jesus lived under that theocracy, but His death and the subsequent dispersal of Israel brought an end to it. By His Spirit working through the early church, it is very clear that He did not mean to perpetuate the theocratic system throughout the whole world. Even at the first council at Jerusalem, they said, "We had a system of laws that we ourselves could not bear, and now we should not try to impose this on the Gentile world" (see Acts 15:10). I believe the church has been acting in accordance with Christ, as He revealed His will through His Spirit to the early church.

THE TASK OF THE CHURCH

I said earlier that modern Christianity is less effective than it could be. I want to explore that further. Indeed, why is much of modern Christianity so impotent? Answer: a deficient view of Christ the King, a view that compartmentalizes our religious life and assigns it artificial boundaries, as opposed to the kingdom of God, which is like yeast that works its way through the whole dough.

Compare, for instance, the number of those who claim to be born-again Christians with those who profess to be homosexuals. The most scientific study to date on sex in America, conducted in the early 1990s under the auspices of the University of Chicago, found that only 2.8 percent of men identified themselves as homosexual or bisexual and only 1.4 percent of women.[21] Contrast that number with those who claim to be born again. George Gallup Jr. reports that 40 percent of Americans claim to be born again. He also reports a more conservative figure of 20 percent who claim to be born again based on a threefold criteria: they have accepted Jesus Christ; they believe the Bible is the Word of God, which we should obey; and they believe we should somehow share our faith.[22] Let us suppose the latter number is correct. You are still talking about a large group of people. This is not taking into account the fact that 78 percent of Americans identify themselves as Christians.[23] For the sake of our argument, let us use Gallup's conservative figure. Even at that, there are nearly ten Christians to every homosexual or lesbian.

Would casual observers of our culture know this? Would they realize it in terms of the political influence of Christians versus homosexuals? Would they know it if they visited a college campus? Would they recognize these things if they read one of the country's daily newspapers? How about the national media? We have the numbers. We have the millions. Most important, we have hope. C. S. Lewis said this about hope: "Hope... means...a continual looking forward to the eternal world.... It does not mean that we are to leave the present world as it is. If you read history you will find that the Christians who did most for the present world were just those who thought most of the next.... It is since Christians have largely ceased to think of the other world that they have become so ineffective in this. Aim at Heaven and you will get earth 'thrown in'; aim at earth and you will get neither."[24]

We must always hope for change and work to influence the world for the better and for the good of the world to come. However, a strong argument for a privatized faith can be made by pointing to what Jesus said in the Sermon on the Mount: that we should not do our holy deeds to be seen by men but that we should pray in private and fast discreetly and give anonymously. That teaching about private faith certainly applies on an individual level, but it does not apply to how we are to serve God by serving our country. We cannot claim this passage as an excuse to shirk our God-given civic duty. Some Christians argue to keep faith private, lest we flaunt our righteousness on street corners, but in reality they lack courage, fearing public rejection or an inability to defend their beliefs and political views from a spiritual basis. Maybe they are too familiar with the kind of scorn heaped on Jerry Falwell even in the days after his death in May 2007.

People will disagree about how Christian morality should inform public policy. But knowing that political views always derive from an internal morality, we must make it our duty to declare publicly what we believe. It is my hope that this book will help you do that.

CONCLUSION

So can anyone be so bold as to say how Jesus would vote? I think the answer is yes. He left us all sorts of commands and principles to follow. Obviously, there is ambiguity in some of those principles; otherwise Christian history would not be full of sincere, well-meaning Christians fighting over those principles, over doctrine. Human pride is a huge factor in such fights. Just as Jesus dealt with religious Pharisees and secular-minded Sadducees, so we contend with both in our time. In declaring Christian principles that guide voting, we cannot help but be controversial. Others will disagree. It goes with the territory. But unless we risk offending, we cannot uphold our duty to God. John Calvin once said, "The task of the church is to make the invisible reign of Christ visible."[25] As we submit to His reign more and more in our lives, and we compromise less and less with the world, we will see powerful results in our land.

Render unto Caesar

Render therefore to Caesar the things that are Caesar's,
and to God the things that are God's.

—MATTHEW 22:21

I n the Gospels we read the story of the religious leaders who asked Jesus whether or not they should pay taxes. It may sound like an unusual question to us, but in their cultural context, the question made sense. One way the Romans oppressed the Jewish nation was by taxing them. They set things up so that individual Jews could betray their own people and become tax collectors. After the tax collectors had exacted the required amount from each family, they could then charge extra in order to make it worth their while. Obviously, these civil servants gained a notorious reputation.

In Jesus's day, a tax collector was right up there (or right down there) with a prostitute. The people were not fans of this oppressive tax system. Nor would we be. A Jewish leader saw an opportunity to turn the people against Jesus with a question about taxes. Here, then, is the passage from Matthew's gospel:

> Then the Pharisees went and plotted how they might entangle
> Him in His talk. And they sent to Him their disciples with the
> Herodians, saying, "Teacher, we know that You are true, and teach
> the way of God in truth; nor do You care about anyone, for You
> do not regard the person of men. Tell us, therefore, what do You
> think? Is it lawful to pay taxes to Caesar, or not?"

But Jesus perceived their wickedness, and said, "Why do you test Me, you hypocrites? Show Me the tax money."

So they brought Him a denarius.

And He said to them, "Whose image and inscription is this?"

They said to Him, "Caesar's."

And He said to them, "Render therefore to Caesar the things that are Caesar's, and to God the things that are God's." When they had heard these words, they marveled, and left Him and went their way. (Matthew 22:15–22)

What does the Bible say about our responsibility as citizens of this country? It is our responsibility to do what good citizenship requires. For us, today, one aspect of giving to Caesar that which is his is through political involvement. There is a relationship between obedience to God's laws and the continuation of a peaceful society. Does it make any difference whether people obey God's laws? Of course it does. Just look at the daily news and witness the vile crimes and ills that plague us. God has judged cities and nations for their wickedness, and we are partly responsible for the places in which we live. Therefore, it is our duty and our responsibility to affect them.

IMPOSING MORALITY?

It is interesting that those who say Christians should have no part in running this nation are quite vociferous about saying we should not "impose our morality" upon them. This statement has been made repeatedly by various public figures, and Christians are often silenced by it. "Oh, yes, I personally believe in such and such, but I can't impose my morality on others." This, of course, must mean that, though my conscience tells me what is right, I must ignore my conscience.

My friend, there is a name for that: hypocrisy. To violate one's conscience is among the most heinous things one can do. Certainly, a life in politics was never intended to require violating our consciences by voting for what is morally repugnant. We must remember that every time a legislature enacts legislation, it is always an imposition of morality. It is ignorant to suggest that the law of the land must be "morality free." Laws against thievery impose the morality of the honest over the dishonest. Laws against prostitution impose a sexual morality upon those who take a different view. Does this cause great indignation to some people? Certainly. In fact, the American Civil Liberties Union (ACLU) has declared that the solicitation of prostitutes is protected speech and thus any laws prohibiting such solicitation are unconstitutional.

Declaring anything legal or illegal is a statement of morality. Legislation is built upon morality, and morality is built upon religion. There is no escaping that fact. Yet today, secular humanists are trying to push Christianity off the field and replace it with their religion of secular humanism, which gives way to its agenda of state-supported immorality. They wish to have their so-called new morality enacted into legislation, and they have succeeded about 50 percent of the time. Let us not be deceived by supposing that this is anything other than an imposition of morality.

Even the U.S. Supreme Court, in a footnote to the 1961 decision of *Torcaso v. Watkins,* said that different ideological systems—including secular humanism—could be defined as religion. So when the Constitution forbids the establishment of a state religion, it includes the establishment of secular humanism. However, because secular humanism claims to be "pure" of religion and morality, those beliefs are being established today.

Rees Lloyd is a former ACLU attorney who now opposes that organization's anti-Christian agenda. He notes that "in *Torcaso v. Watkins,* the U.S. Supreme Court said that secular humanism is a religion—it's a religion without a deity, like Buddhism, Taoism—but it's a religion. Well, what happens if secularism drives all other religion out of the public square? Isn't that governmental endorsement of a religion, the name of which is atheistic secularism? I believe it is."[1]

Bill Federer, an author and expert on America's Christian heritage, points out: "When groups say they just want the government…to be neutral, when it comes to religion, really what they're saying is: we want your belief system out and we want our belief system in. We want your thoughts out and we want our thoughts to be the thoughts that underlie the actions of the government. And so, when groups like the ACLU say that, they need to be called on the carpet, because they are actually promoting a state religion of secular humanism."

One of the things Federer found was in the U.S. Supreme Court case *Abington Township v. Schempp.* In 1963 the Court said, "The state may not establish a religion of secularism in the sense of affirmatively opposing or showing hostility to religion, thus preferring those who believe in no religion over those that do believe. Refusal to permit religious exercises, thus, is seen not as the realization of state neutrality, but rather, the establishment of a religion of secularism."[2] In a later decision at a lower level, the U.S. District Court for the Western District of Virginia stated in 1983: "The First Amendment was never intended to insulate our public institutions from any mention of God, the Bible or religion. When such insulation occurs, another religion, such as secular humanism, is effectively established. Clearly, the Establishment Clause can be violated in this regard without a showing of outright hostility to traditional theistic religions."[3]

In opposing any Christian involvement in the public arena and by insisting on supposed "neutrality," humanists impose their nonreligion on our nation.

THE GOAL OF THE FOUNDING FATHERS

Secular humanism is a far cry from the views of the Founding Fathers of this country. The great Daniel Webster said, "Let us not forget the religious character of our origin. Our Fathers were brought hither by their veneration of the Christian religion. They journeyed by its light, and labored in its hope. They sought to incorporate its principles with the element of their society, and to diffuse its influence through all their institutions in the full conviction that this is the happiest society which partakes in the highest degree of the mild and peaceful spirit of Christianity."[4]

Samuel Adams, who has sometimes been called the "Firebrand of the Revolution," said, "The rights of colonists as Christians...may be best understood by reading and carefully studying the institutes of the great Lawgiver and Head of the Christian church, which are to be found clearly written and promulgated in the New Testament."[5]

George Washington said, "While just government protects all in their religious rights, true religion affords to government its surest support."[6]

John Quincy Adams summed it up by saying, "The highest glory of the American Revolution was this: it connected in one indissoluble bond, the principles of civil government with the principles of Christianity."[7]

These statements are a far cry from the comments of modern secularists who view religious involvement in the political arena as a threat to the happiness and well-being of our republic. Busily engaged in pouring the acids of their unbelief upon that indissoluble bond, they are hoping to totally remove the principles of Christianity from our nation.

Many years ago the Arthur DeMoss Foundation placed full-page ads in newspapers all over the country, quoting a number of the Founding Fathers and making this statement: "Religion's influence on public policy has had a long and distinguished history. Over the past 200 years religion has been a stabilizing force in this country. Suddenly Americans are being told that religion and morality were never meant to influence politics. To believe this would require a disregard for our history...even the desertion of the principles of our forefathers."

The values of religion and morality have influenced public policy from our beginning to our present. Do we now separate religion from politics and ignore our nation's heritage? Think about it. Secularists quote Founding Fathers such as Washington as if he supported their agenda. In truth, though, Washington said, "Of all the dispositions and habits which lead to political prosperity, Religion and morality are indispensable supports."[8]

Daniel Webster noted, "Our ancestors established their system of government on morality and religious sentiment."[9] And so it has been down through the years.

In 1828 Supreme Court Justice Joseph Story, who wrote the great commentaries on the Constitution, said this:

Probably at the time of the adoption of the Constitution, and of the amendment to it now under consideration [First Amendment], the general if not universal sentiment in America was, that Christianity ought to receive encouragement from the State so far as it was not incompatible with the private rights of conscience and the freedom of religious worship. An attempt to level all religions, and to make it a matter of state policy to hold all in utter indifference, would have created universal disapprobation, if not universal indignation....

The real object of the First Amendment was not to countenance, much less to advance, Mahometanism, or Judaism, or infidelity, by prostrating Christianity; but to exclude all rivalry among Christian sects, and to prevent any national ecclesiastical establishment which should give to a hierarchy the exclusive patronage of the national government.[10]

They established a nation here that allowed tremendous freedom. "Many [immigrants] have come since those days," said the great nineteenth-century theologian Charles Hodge of Princeton.

All are welcomed; all are admitted to equal rights and privileges. All are allowed to acquire property, whatever their religious feelings, and to vote in every election, made eligible to all offices and invested with equal influence in all public affairs. All are allowed to worship as they please, or not to worship at all, if they see fit. No man is molested for his religion or for his want of religion. No man is required to profess any form of faith, or to join any religious association. More than this cannot reasonably be demanded. More, however, is demanded. The atheist demands that the government should be conducted on the principle that Christianity is false. The atheist demands that it should be conducted on the assumption that there is no God. And the positivist on the principle that man is not a free moral agent.... The sufficient answer to all this is that it cannot possibly be done.[11]

No, the founders of this nation had a very different view from what is being told to us today. Unfortunately, Christians have inherited by default a glorious patrimony, and they have allowed it to sift through their fingers like sand, until now we find ourselves in a great struggle even to maintain and hold on to the glorious inheritance we have in this country. Add in those even within the Christian camp who have said, in effect, the opposite of the classic hymn "Rise Up, O Men of God":

> Sit down, O men of God
> His kingdom *He* will bring,
> Whenever it may please His will.
> You cannot do a thing.

Just a few decades ago it was reported that 50 percent of Christians were not even registered to vote, and 50 percent of those who were registered did not vote. I'm reminded of the old anecdote about two Christians. One of them said, "The main problems in our nation today are ignorance and apathy, don't you agree?" The other replied, "I don't know, and I don't care."

Fortunately, that attitude may be passing away, and people are realizing that we are to serve not only the kingdom of God but to render unto Caesar the things that are Caesar's. I thank God that the church is waking up and the men and women of God are facing their responsibilities. God has given our magistrates their positions and to us the country and its laws. Not all rulers are just, nor are all laws. So as much as it is up to us, we must attempt to bring about positive change where we can.

THE CHRISTIAN'S HIGHEST DUTY

Let me say first what I do not believe: I do not believe that we should have an established state church in America. I think the idea is abhorrent, even if it were a Presbyterian church. I do not believe we should have a church state. I do not believe that preachers should endorse candidates from the pulpit, even though that is perfectly legal. I do not believe that preachers should become embroiled in partisan politics.

In fifty years I have not, to my knowledge, ever mentioned the name of either one of those political parties whose names I will not mention now, or I could not make that statement again. Lastly, I do not think preachers should tell people for whom they should vote. I do believe, however, that it is incumbent upon us as ministers of the Word of God to declare the principles and moral teachings of the Scripture that apply to public policy in this country.

It was from the pulpits of New England that great proclamations thundered forth concerning liberty and freedom and the sovereignty of God and the nature of man, proclamations that ultimately led to the foundation of our Constitution and the American Revolution. Historians agree on that fact. And that still remains the job of the pulpit.

I must say this to you: it is a sin *not* to vote. After I made that remark from the pulpit many years ago, someone said to me following the service, "Where does it say in the Bible that it is a sin not to vote?" Well, sit still, I am going to tell you right now. Jesus Christ said this: "Render therefore to Caesar the things that are Caesar's." That means we are to render unto the state whatever it is our responsibility as citizens of the state to render. And certainly, in this nation, that includes at the very minimum that we should vote.

Now, I said before that there may be times when no candidate can be supported in good conscience. But aside from such times, if you do not render to Caesar your obligation as a citizen of this country, my friend, it is a sin. I hope the day will come when Christians will look upon apathy and indifference concerning their responsibilities as Christian citizens in this great nation as a base and iniquitous thing, and they should be ashamed to admit that they have failed to live up to their duty.

Yet Jesus's statement also includes the reality that nothing is Caesar's apart from God. We should render him nothing if we do not render it as part of our responsibility to God. We should not assume Jesus is saying that all money ultimately belongs to Caesar, because Caesar controlled the monetary system as a man-made construct, but we should pay taxes on the money as Jesus commanded. And we should certainly take part in promoting Christian responsibility to the political systems to which we are responsible.

This is just one aspect of fulfilling our duty to the Great Commission of Jesus Christ, to take the gospel to every living creature. We must not only be the light of the world, bringing the gospel to those who are perishing in darkness and ignorance, but we must also be the salt of the earth, exercising its privileges in the kingdom of Caesar to prevent the nation from corrupting altogether. The very first charter given to the very first settlers in this nation was the 1606 Virginia Charter, which laid out the purposes for the Jamestown landing in 1607. The document recorded that the colonists came to Jamestown for the "propagating of Christian religion to such people as yet live in darkness and miserable ignorance of the true knowledge and worship of God."[12] My friend, today it is not the Native Americans who live in utter darkness and ignorance of the true worship of God. It is our job to propagate the Christian religion to all Americans, to all people. That is our high and glorious calling. By the grace of God, may we do it.

IS THERE A CURE?

What is the cure? It can be nothing other than a return to God. We have turned our backs upon God, and we need to return to Him. A historian has said that never in the history of the world has any nation in so brief a span of time turned its back upon its God, upon its religion, upon its morals, upon its ethics, upon its traditions, and upon its culture.

I think about a church near Houston—a church of twelve hundred people in a town of thirty thousand—and they said, "Enough is enough," and they became active. They had not been before. What happened? When they became active, three of the city's five commissioners were members of this church. Three of the five people on the board of education were members of this church. So were the attorney general, the mayor, and many other civic leaders. All kinds of leaders of that community are members of that church, and they continue to transform their city for good.

Gary Bauer, a great man of God and a great American, wrote a small book entitled *Our Hopes, Our Dreams,* which reveals the results of some studies by his organization on what would happen if Christians reclaimed America. He said that from the state house to the White House, from the local courts to the Supreme Court, and throughout the education system—the whole kettle of fish—the results were so astonishingly positive that even unbelievers, when presented with the results, were very favorably impressed. Can you imagine what it would mean to this country?

Christians need to get involved. If every Christian in America merely registered and voted, that would make a tremendous difference in the politics of communities as well as the nation.

Might I also suggest that it would be best for you to vote for Christians. Now you say, "That sounds very discriminatory. You shouldn't say that." I am merely quoting John Jay, the first chief justice of the first Supreme Court, appointed by George Washington, and one of the great founders of this country. He, along with Madison and Hamilton, wrote *The Federalist Papers,* which persuaded the colonies to ratify the Constitution. Jay said, "It is the duty as well as the privilege and interest of our Christian nation to select and prefer Christians for their rulers."[13]

One of our problems is that we do not have enough of them running for office to even "prefer." Maybe God is speaking to you.

Also, we need to be involved in sharing the gospel of Christ with people. You cannot impose a Christian culture on a godless society. Dear friend, to my dying breath I will be urging you to share the good news of Christ with others. It is the responsibility of everyone who claims to be a follower of Jesus.

Have you been doing that? Do you realize that just by inviting people to church, you could change this country? They might hear the gospel, and their hearts could be changed. That is what it's all about. I believe we can see an enormous change for the better in this nation in the next decade if *we* will become faithful to what God has told us to do.

One of my favorite statesmen is a congressman from the St. Louis area: Todd Akin. He is a seminary graduate and has chosen politics as his ministry. He once said this about our duty as Christians: if each Christian took seriously his own little piece of turf that God has given him, we would see the land transformed. While rendering to Caesar, we must remember that ultimately we are rendering to God. Our duty is to share His message and influence people in the public sector, not only through political involvement, but also through the ultimate "political espionage," namely, evangelism.

CONCLUSION

I pray we may begin today to determine that we are going to be salt in a corrupting body politic. May we determine that we are going to bring the light of the gospel into the darkness of a lost world, that the good news of

Jesus Christ may ring out again, and that the tidings of salvation and eternal life will become the blessed possession and privilege and joy of people across this nation. If so, this country will change to a cleaner, safer, and kinder place to live. May it be, and may it begin with you and me.

Salt and Light

You are the salt of the earth;
but if the salt loses its flavor, how shall it be seasoned?
It is then good for nothing but to be thrown out
and trampled underfoot by men.
You are the light of the world.
A city that is set on a hill cannot be hidden.
Nor do they light a lamp and put it under a basket,
but on a lampstand, and it gives light
to all who are in the house.
Let your light so shine before men,
that they may see your good works
and glorify your Father in heaven.

—MATTHEW 5:13–16

If you live in Florida, you get to be pretty familiar with the phenomenon of the hurricane, and you quickly learn there are two things essential to have a hurricane. You have to have winds circulating at rapid speed, and you have to have a calm, warm center, where nothing is really happening. Once I walked out of my house into the eye of a hurricane (not recommended) and looked up at the stars. It was absolutely still; there was no wind, no howling, no nothing. It was beautiful, and yet it is the heat of that warm center that feeds those destructive winds. Meteorologists show us pictures of these swirling winds and then say, "You see, right here an eye is beginning to develop." Yes, my friend, the moving current of air has become a hurricane. And then the winds pick up, a storm forms, and a tremendous, unpredictable power is unleashed.

Hurricane Andrew demonstrated that when it roamed across southern Miami in 1992 with winds of 160 to 180 miles an hour and changed everything. There were not merely branches and palm fronds strewn all over the region; there was steel, aluminum, and blocks of concrete scattered everywhere. Andrew cut a twenty-five-mile swath across the whole southern peninsula of Florida. More recently, Hurricanes Charley, Frances, Ivan, Jean, Katrina, and Wilma wreaked various levels of devastation, demonstrating the same principles.

I see a lesson in hurricanes that applies to religion. Piety is personal godliness, whereas pietism is piety as the end-all, be-all. Pietism is like the eye of a hurricane. In pietism, you have the gospel—the warm, quiet heart—but all the winds have disappeared. You have the warm center but no power. Pietism passes through and leaves unchanged all that it touches.

First, we need to ask ourselves if we are truly discipling and equipping our people to evangelize, to confidently and graciously share the gospel in an effective way. How many people have you trained thusly in your church? Second, are we fulfilling the cultural mandates as John Calvin, John Knox, John Piper, and others in the Calvinistic tradition stressed so much, or have we become pietists?

Now piety is a wonderful thing, but pietism is a negation of the work of the church. Similarly, I'm all in favor of the feminine, but feminism is a curse. What are we? Where are we going? What tracks are we traveling on? I remember a few years ago when Don Wildmon said something that struck me as profound:

★ Today four thousand innocent babies had their lives snuffed out, and three hundred thousand pulpits were silent.

★ The television networks make a mockery of Christians, of the Christian faith, and of Christian values, and three hundred thousand pulpits are silent.

★ Violence, sexual immorality, and perversion of every kind have become standard fare on television, in movies, and on radio, and still three hundred thousand pulpits are silent.

★ Teenage suicide is at the highest that it has ever been; rape has increased 700 percent, and three hundred thousand pulpits are silent.

★ Rock and rap fill our airways and the minds of our children with lyrics that legitimize and glorify rape and murder, forced sex, sadomasochism, sodomy, and every other kind of evil, and three hundred thousand pulpits are silent.[1]

Are we really equipping our people to evangelize? Are we fulfilling the cultural mandates to change the culture for Christ? to bring glory to His Name? We sing "This Is My Father's World." But do we really believe that? Would He even own it today? Is your pulpit silent?

For five summers in a row, while on study leave in California, visiting church after church, I listened for a word on our world from a Christian perspective, including politics, but I never heard one. This is a time for reflection and perhaps reassessment of where we are going. We confess that all of us have sinned and fallen short of what God would have us to be. We confess that we, like all the rest, have failed to be what Jesus would have His pastors to be. We pray that Christ grants us boldness and deliverance from our fear and our timidity so we will not leave a godless, pagan world to our children. Recently the governors of Scotland declared: Scotland is now a pagan nation. That is not what John Knox and the other reformers fought so valiantly for. We should not let our forefathers' work end in vain.

A CHRISTIAN WORLD-AND-LIFE VIEW

We are to be salt in this world as well as light. Virtually all Christians recognize they have some responsibility to spread the Christian message—to be light in the darkness. However, not all Christians recognize their role as salt in society.

I believe we can learn some important principles from the great and humble sixteenth-century reformer of Geneva, John Calvin, who made a significant contribution to Western civilization, namely, the development of a biblically reformed world-and-life view structured along the principle of sphere sovereignty. In addition to sharing our faith, applying our faith to all of life is the other track that the gospel train is supposed to run on. As Jesus said, we are not only to be the light of the world, we are to be the salt of the earth. To witness for Christ is the Great Commission. To be salt for Christ is called many things, sometimes the "cultural mandate," sometimes the "dominion mandate." Whatever it is called, we are to impact our culture for Christ in every facet while we are here in this world.

Think of the phrase *cultural mandate.* Former Calvin College professor, H. Henry Meeter wrote, "Culture is just another name for the duty of mankind to develop the raw materials of this world as found in nature and in man himself, to demonstrate the great possibilities inherent in creation, which the Creator has put there, and make them serve the purpose which God has intended they should."[2]

What is called the cultural mandate is simply the redemption, not only of men, but of all the works of man that are called culture. This includes all that man has created and has, so this is to impact every facet of man's life in this world. That is the cultural mandate we are to perform as well as the Great Commission. Those are the two goals that the church—every church, every pastor, every Christian—should be aiming to fulfill.

This was the great goal of Calvin. The man was not only a theologian and educator, but some commentators have noted that he was also a social statesman. History professor W. S. Reid writes of Calvin: "Many of his ideas in politics, aesthetics, science, and history became so interwoven in Western thought that we must recognize him as one of the great seminal minds, one of the formative factors in the development of Western culture and civilization."[3] Calvin endeavored, as a reformer and as the dominant influence in Geneva, to realize the ideal Christian commonwealth in that city-state based on the ideals he found in Scripture. In the end Calvin successfully transformed the city of Geneva into a Christian commonwealth, which John Knox called "the greatest school of Christ since the time of the apostles."

The great reformers included:

★ Calvin, who transformed Geneva

★ Knox, who transformed every facet of Scotland into a school of Christ

★ the Puritans who made their part of America into a Christian commonwealth

★ Abraham Kuyper, who labored indefatigably, producing more than two hundred large volumes of work and editing a daily paper in Amsterdam, started the Free University, and did scores of other things. His enemies thought he had twenty hands as he worked so diligently to transform Holland into a Christian commonwealth. He was not afraid to get his hands dirty, and he changed that country.

★ Francis Schaeffer, who preached one of his last sermons in our pulpit (Coral Ridge Presbyterian, Fort Lauderdale) and talked about the need for Christians to be involved in the culture and not let the culture go to hell because it was left to unbelievers

How we love to rejoice in the great things that our forebears—the great Calvinistic forebears—accomplished in every sphere of society. We think of how they were able to get rid of slavery, how they changed the insane asylums, how they uplifted the estate of women, how they so incredibly blessed the condition of children, and one thing after another and another in America.

When the first abolition society was formed, eight of the first ten members of that society were not merely Christians or Calvinists; they were clergymen laboring to end the curse of slavery in America. It was a Christian in England (William Wilberforce) who had done the same thing only a few years before. These were people who realized that redemption was the redemption of the whole of creation, that Christ came into the world to destroy the works of the devil, and those works are not only in individual hearts and minds but they are in the fruits and labors and the developments of those people.

We live in a country today where Christ gets little or no glory. We see that the whole counsel of God must include a well-developed sociology, a transformation of the institutions of men. If we are going to see the redemption of the earth, it is going to involve not just people but the works of their hands as well. What a different place this country would be.

Do you realize that in 1850 virtually every daily newspaper in America was run by evangelical Christians? The editorials frequently quoted the Bible. Columnists wrote about Scripture and about theological questions. Every week a sermon by a noted cleric was published in the papers. Today who can name one daily newspaper in America that is run by Christians on Christian principles and quotes Christian texts? We have abandoned our culture.

The basic working principle of such a cultural view is called, as all the clergymen and probably a few of the laymen should know, a *Weltanschauung*. What does the German word mean? It translates as "world-and-life view." How many of you have a Weltanschauung?

I have discovered that, percentage-wise, not many professing Christians have a Weltanschauung. I recall when I was converted, I went to a church for the first time. I had not been there two weeks when they asked me to teach the young adults' Sunday-school class. I did not know anything about the

Bible other than the Jews came to Egypt and lived in the land of Goshen. It occurred to me that what I was reading about Naboth's vineyard and Ahab might have taken place on Mars, for all I knew. Then, a year or so later, when I became a bit more acquainted with the New Testament, I really wondered if all of that actually happened. I say again, do we have a Weltanschauung?

You may remember hearing about the beginning of a movement called pietism back in the 1700s. It began in Germany in a rather formalistic Lutheran church with Jacob Spener (1635–1705), a very pious, godly man who believed that something was missing from life. He defined that missing element as personal piety in response to the gospel. He stressed that, in palingenesis (what we would call being "born again"), it was essential to incorporate regular prayer, Scripture reading, church attendance, and quiet personal pursuits, like family and child rearing. That was an important, vital development in the church, but new generations distorted these teachings. The pietism movement became not just an important foundation for Christian service; it became the focus of Christian service, and acts of Christian service and duty to society fell away.

Salt preserves, but if salt loses its saltiness, it is worthless.

CONCLUSION

We are not called to be the vinegar of the world; neither are we called to be the sugar. We are called to be salt, which not only preserves but also purifies and promotes healing. Like salt water to a throat, as every speaker and singer knows, we should not simply sting, but we should be a clarifying element that allows the deeper Word to speak.

Finally, salt seasons, bringing out the natural zest and flavor of the bread of life. Let us aspire to exhibit all our diverse characteristics for the good of our country through performing our duty to the God we serve.

Part II
THE ISSUES

Matters of Life and Death

Abortion, Stem Cells, Suicide, and Euthanasia

I have come that they may have life,
and that they may have it more abundantly.

—John 10:10

There is probably not a more controversial subject dividing Americans than the issue of abortion. At the same time, I believe there is not another subject where the stakes for Christian voters are so high or the moral contrasts so clear.

Abortion has been a central issue for Bible-believing Christians in the decades since the U.S. Supreme Court made the procedure legal in its shocking *Roe v. Wade* decision. But abortion is only the best known of a number of issues that I call matters of life and death. The others include stem-cell research, suicide, and euthanasia. Because the theological debates surrounding these life issues are based on similar sets of concerns, we will examine abortion first and in greater length before examining the other issues.

The clear biblical teaching is that God is the giver of life; it is created by Him and is, therefore, sacred. Life and death are in His hands.

The starting point for our discussions on these issues is the strong and consistent biblical testimony in support of life. True, the Bible does not include the word *abortion*. But if the New Testament teaches us anything, it was how Jesus Christ declared that we must reach out and be concerned for our neighbors and for the world in which we live. Christians must have a greater concern than simply personal peace and prosperity. Let us start by examining a handful of Scriptures on the issue of life.

THUS SAYS THE LORD

In Psalm 139 David gives a lengthy explanation of how God knit him together in his mother's womb and how he was miraculously designed— as an unborn child:

> For You formed my inward parts;
>
> You covered me in my mother's womb.
>
> I will praise You, for I am fearfully and wonderfully made;
>
> Marvelous are Your works,
>
> And that my soul knows very well. (Psalm 139:13–14)

Unborn children are not merely masses of tissue. Though the human body, even at the unborn level, was greater than earlier generations could comprehend, modern science now verifies what David poetically described. Lehigh University Professor Michael Behe, author of *Darwin's Black Box,* once told my coauthor, Jerry Newcombe, in a radio interview that if we were to compile all the information found in the *simplest cell* of the human body into volumes the size of the *Encyclopaedia Britannica,* the information would comprise two to three dozen such volumes.[1] Furthermore, our bodies contain trillions and trillions of cells. Indeed, we are fearfully and wonderfully made.

In Jeremiah 1 the weeping prophet received his prophetic call. Here, again, God reveals His high view of human life:

> Then the word of the LORD came to me, saying:
>
>> "Before I formed you in the womb I knew you;
>>
>> Before you were born I sanctified you;
>>
>> I ordained you a prophet to the nations." (Jeremiah 1:4–5)

The unborn is a human being in the making, and human beings are made in the image of God. In the New Testament, we read of this incident from Luke:

> Now Mary arose in those days and went into the hill country with haste, to a city of Judah, and entered the house of Zacharias and greeted Elizabeth. And it happened, when Elizabeth heard the greeting of Mary, that the babe leaped in her womb. (Luke 1:39–41)

The "babe"—not even "unborn babe"—is the word *brephos,* which is used for both the unborn child and the young child lying in a manger. Masses of tissue do not leap for joy.

The Bible famously declares in the Ten Commandments: "Thou shalt not kill" (Exodus 20:13, KJV), which is better translated "You shall not murder." Surely the deliberate killing of an unborn child could be viewed as murder—although in our politically correct age, we do not like to say this.

"LIFE" OR "CHOICE"

In the heated debates between people supporting the pro-life and pro-choice positions, many on the pro-choice side cite Exodus 21, arguing that it suggests that taking the life of an unborn child is not the same as taking the life of a born human being:

> If men fight, and hurt a woman with child, so that she gives birth prematurely, yet no harm follows, he shall surely be punished accordingly as the woman's husband imposes on him; and he shall pay as the judges determine. But if any harm follows, then you

shall give life for life, eye for eye, tooth for tooth, hand for hand, foot for foot, burn for burn, wound for wound, stripe for stripe. (Exodus 21:22–25)

However, the Bible draws a huge distinction between the *deliberate* and *accidental* taking of life. In this particular case, justice demands a life (the adult who accidentally caused the injury) for a life (the unborn child). This passage says nothing about the *deliberate destruction* of the unborn.

In Proverbs 6, the Lord lists seven things that He condemns, among them, "hands that shed innocent blood" (Proverbs 6:17). I believe abortions fall into this category. Who is more innocent than an unborn baby?

One last passage to touch on is in the prologue of John's gospel: "In the beginning was the Word, and the Word was with God, and the Word was God.... And the Word became flesh and dwelt among us, and we beheld His glory, the glory as of the only begotten of the Father, full of grace and truth" (John 1:1, 14). When Jesus, who existed from the beginning, entered our world of time, space, and history, He did so as an unborn baby. Though in His ministry Jesus did not directly address abortion, He affirmed the truth and reliability of the Word of God, and both the Old and New Testaments affirm the humanity of the unborn.

The Judeo-Christian ethical tradition stands in stark contrast to pre-Christian worldviews that granted comparatively little protection to the unborn and the young. The ancient religions of the Persians, the Greeks, and the Romans had little concern for the sanctity of life. Babies were not only aborted in the womb, but if they lived to be born and were unwanted, they were exposed to the elements and left to die. In some cases children were sacrificed on pagan altars.

Let me quote a profound statement by the late Malcolm Muggeridge, the brilliant English author:

The sanctity of life is, of course, a religious or transcendental concept, and has no meaning otherwise; if there is no God, life cannot have sanctity. By the same token, the quality of life is an earthly or worldly concept, and can only be expressed legalistically, and in materialistic terms; the soul does not come into it.[2]

POWERFUL RESEARCH FROM SOUTH DAKOTA

During the 2006 election, a well-funded abortion-promoting political action group (PAC) donated thousands of dollars for abortion-rights candidates. When contrasted with the pro-life candidates, who had far less money, they did not fare nearly as well. Steven Ertelt, editor of LifeNews.com, wrote: "In a statement provided to LifeNews.com the National Right to Life Committee said it was involved in 87 highly contested races for the House and Senate and the group won 53 percent of those contests."[3] Furthermore, a pro-life group, the Susan B. Anthony List, reported that 59 percent of the national-level candidates they supported won. In contrast, Emily's List, which is "the leading pro-abortion political action committee,"[4] won only 43 percent of its national candidates. Ertelt quoted a National Right to Life spokesperson, who said, "Without the outstanding efforts of pro-lifers the results [of the 2006 elections] would have been far more tragic for the pro-life movement."[5]

It is interesting to note that in the same year, the South Dakota legislature proposed a law banning abortion. It did not pass, but the research they conducted involved studying the side effects of abortion since 1973, the year the U.S. Supreme Court announced its *Roe v. Wade* decision. The bipartisan task force consisted of seventeen people, including several who called themselves pro-choice. They collected thirty-five hundred pages of scientific research, heard from fifty-eight experts, national and international, who compiled research studies both for and against, and collected thousands of affidavits from women who had abortions, and then compressed all the data into a seventy-one-page document.[6]

Drs. Allen Unruh and Leslee Unruh of South Dakota organized this. Allen summarized the findings of the task force to study abortion:

We found out that there's basically very little information given to women prior to an abortion, and what is given is false. The "informed consent" that they receive is a four-minute cassette, a message by an abortionist on tape. There's no opportunity to ask questions. And they're assigned a number, and as long as they have a number, they've been "informed of abortion." And in this message it says, "Your chances of dying are seven times greater, 700% higher, if you have the baby than if we terminate your pregnancy." And they tell women there are no side effects emotionally. The only emotion you will experience is relief. And the abortion counselor has no training in counseling, no [master's] in counseling, no doctorate degrees, no psychiatry, psychology, or ministerial background. They're only trained on how to sell abortion.[7]

The task force also found that many women who "choose" abortion do so because of pressure exerted on them by parents, boyfriends, or husbands:

Nobody skips into an abortion clinic. They do not look forward to it like a chocolate sundae. And then they're forced into an abortion. In fact, one of the women that testified before us said her mother told her she had to have an abortion. When she was in the waiting room, she started crying. She said, "I can't do it. I change my mind. I can't do it." And they called the mother, and she told them, "You have to do this abortion." So they said, "Come in this other room; we're gonna calm you down," and they injected something in her, and when she woke up, they said, "The abortion's over. Is there anything else you'd like?" She said, "Yes, do you have a gun?" And you can imagine the trauma involved.[8]

The task force paid special attention to two thousand women who had had abortions, concluding: "Of these post-abortive women, over 99% of them testified that abortion is destructive of the rights, interests, and health of women and that abortion should not be legal."[9]

STEM-CELL RESEARCH

There is a great deal of confusion over the issue of stem-cell research, which typically refers to *embryonic*-stem-cell research conducted on the cells of human embryos. While supporters of the research claim it is needed to combat human illnesses, the research has not yet yielded any cures. (However, *adult*-stem-cell research, which does not raise the ethical issues surrounding embryonic research, *has* yielded profitable results.)

Why then do some promote stem-cell research so vigorously? At least one reason is money; researchers may be able to patent cures found through the research. As one chapter of the National Right to Life organization pointed out: "Some biotechnology firms are hoping that they will be able to clone human embryos with specific traits, patent them and then collect royalties from other biotechnology companies who hope to use these embryos or clones of the embryos."[10]

I share the hopes of those who long for cures to human ills. But should human life be expendable in the quest of such cures? Too often, stem-cell research involves creating a new life only to kill it in the interests of research. I believe this is a violation of the Bible's ethics on life.

Politicians who support embryonic-stem-cell research have tugged at our heartstrings by bringing out celebrities like Christopher Reeves and Michael J. Fox to plead their cause. And yet, adult-stem-cell research, in which a living person's stem cells are used, poses no threat to human life. Noted scientist Michael Fumento observed, "Adult stem cells cure and treat more than 70 diseases and are involved in almost 1,300 human clinical trials."[11]

Another thing to remember about the political debate is that the research remains legal. Current policies merely prevent the government from using *public* money to support embryonic-stem-cell research. Scientists are free to pursue embryonic-stem-cell research if they fund it themselves.

Yet to kill the unborn, the most vulnerable among us, defies the Creator and His creation. To kill embryonic stem cells is crossing a line that I believe the Creator would not want us to cross. To do so is to accept the humanist view of man (resulting from random, blind forces) versus the view of man as a special creation.[12]

"RIGHTS" VS. WRONGS: EUTHANASIA AND SUICIDE

Have you noticed we are becoming a throwaway society? Instead of repairing our cameras or refrigerators, we throw them out. And in many cases, manufacturers actually design their products to be irreparable.

Unfortunately, human beings are increasingly being included among those "things" some in our society want to throw away.

The seriousness of devaluating human life can be seen in the fact that the Nazi Holocaust, with all of its incredible atrocities, can be traced back to a very small beginning: the blurring of the line between healing and killing by physicians. Before the Nazis killed the Jews, they began to systematically kill the chronically sick. What do you do about those who are not going to get well? That may seem like a little thing, but historians confirm that it was the first step down a slippery slope that led to Auschwitz.[13]

In talking about Jack Kevorkian (a.k.a. "Dr. Death"), Dr. Charles Krauthammer summarized: "How then to draw the line? Easy. Doctors must not kill. The bright line must be drawn precisely between passive and active measures."[14] In other words, a doctor must uphold the Hippocratic oath to do no harm.

Today many people are blinded to the eternal and divine considerations on these important matters of life and death. However, God has made it very clear: "You shall not murder" (Exodus 20:13). We shall not commit murder of our neighbor, our brother, our mother, our father, or ourselves. We are not our own.

On the matter of suicide, Charles Hodge, perhaps the greatest theologian America ever produced and an incredible scholar of the Bible, expressed it this way: "Suicide is, therefore, self murder. It is the desertion of the pot which God has assigned us."[15]

This does not mean that those who are essentially dead should be kept "alive" indefinitely through artificial means. However, food and water (even if administered through a feeding tube) do not constitute artificial means. By "artificial means," I am talking about keeping a person's body alive by a battery of machines when an individual is not even conscious. We must use the life principle to guide all these decisions and to guide us in how we vote on all these issues.

Each year around January 22 (the anniversary of *Roe v. Wade*), National Sanctity of Human Life Sunday is recognized. At an observance, President George W. Bush declared, "Our nation was built on a promise of life and liberty for all citizens. Guided by a deep respect for human dignity, our Founding Fathers worked to secure these rights for future generations, and today we continue to seek to fulfill their promise in our laws and our society."[16]

Years earlier Francis Schaeffer spoke from the pulpit at Coral Ridge Presbyterian Church. He said that, of all the inalienable rights, life is by far the most important. We should not open a door to practices in our society that remove this fundamental right from those who are vulnerable and in need of our care and compassion.

In these important issues of abortion, embryonic-stem-cell research, suicide, and euthanasia, the great divide is between those who believe man is a special creation of God and those who believe he is just the product of time and chance.

FORGIVENESS IN MERCY

I have no doubt that some readers of this book have participated in an abortion either as a mother, father, friend, or loved one. Though abortion is a sin, I want to assure you that there is mercy with the Lord. There is forgiveness. Some of you have been carrying around guilt and maybe have experienced depression. The Lord is kind and merciful to all of those who will come to Him. Go to Him.

Abortion and other life issues are more than matters of votes and public policy. If you have acted on behalf of death instead of life, confess this to Him and ask Him to cleanse you, to remove the darkness, and to fill you with His joy. He will do that.

One other thing you can do about abortion is to share the gospel with others. They do not need to be contemplating an abortion. Did you ever think that bringing another person to Christ will help get rid of abortion? When people are converted, they begin to adopt the Bible's pro-life outlook. When we love Him, we love life, for He is the giver of life.

CONCLUSION

So how would Jesus vote? He certainly would vote against the destruction of innocent, unborn babies. I believe He would have us vote pro-life, favoring life at all levels of the spectrum.

Suppose I know a candidate is for the pro-choice position. My response is that I cannot support that person. Period. That's because I believe this one issue of life trumps all others. Even if a pro-abortion-rights politician claims to be a Christian, I cannot support him or her in good conscience. (However, left with a choice between one pro-choice candidate and another, one could argue for voting for the lesser of two evils).

As the number of Christians in this country continues to grow, I believe we will see abortion abolished in America. Abortion is a great blotch on the recent history of this country, just as Nazism is a blotch on the past of Germany. The abolition of abortion will happen, but for evil to prevail, the only thing necessary is for good people to do nothing. So we need to vote for godly candidates. Meanwhile, we should do everything in our power to bolster a culture of life.

Crime and Punishment

Judging the Death Penalty

For rulers are not a terror to good works,
but to evil.
Do you want to be unafraid of the authority?
Do what is good, and you will have praise from the same.
For he is God's minister to you for good.
But if you do evil, be afraid;
for he does not bear the sword in vain;
for he is God's minister, an avenger
to execute wrath on him who practices evil.

—ROMANS 13:3–4

How would Jesus vote—or how would Jesus have us vote—when it comes to the death penalty? Some Christians oppose the death penalty under all circumstances. Other believers argue that the death penalty can be appropriate in some circumstances. However, many people are justifiably concerned that some criminal codes have been extremely harsh and cruel and that some people have been executed because of faulty evidence, poor legal help, or their skin color.

For the last several decades, there has been a move in our culture toward a less vindictive and vengeful approach to dealing with criminals. The old concept of "an eye for an eye and a life for a life" has been slowly passing, being replaced with a more merciful approach. Of course one hopes for constructive change in the wrongdoer—to cure the offender and deter him from future crimes. From this perspective, capital punishment is a practice that must inevitably go, for it is absolutely true that capital punishment has never cured anyone. Furthermore, many have argued there is no definite evidence that it deters murder. The question to be faced is this: is the criminal sick and needing a cure, or is he guilty and needing to be punished?

What shall we say about this relatively modern approach to capital punishment? I think, on the surface, it has a tremendous appeal—a real, emotional appeal. We do not *like* to see anyone killed. We have no desire to see anyone placed in the electric chair or given a lethal injection.

But before we come to a conclusion about which view we should support, we need to understand some of the great issues involved in this decision, issues that underlie the whole subject, issues of which most people are completely unaware.

CONFLICTING VIEWS OF LAW

Many of the laws that are part of our national life spring from Judeo-Christian concepts of right and wrong, including the Ten Commandments. But today in the Western world, we are involved in a tremendous legal revolution. Dr. Hebden Taylor, in his excellent book *The New Legality,* states: "The separation of religion from law is rather the separation of Christianity from law. Christianity has for centuries been the major impetus to legal codes, and Western law has been a manifestation of changing and developing currents of Christian philosophy and theology. Now, however, Christianity is in radical and revolutionary process of disestablishment as the religious foundation of laws, states, and civil governments, and it is being steadily replaced by another religion, the religion of humanity or humanism. The fact that humanism is a non-theistic faith does not make it any the less a religion."[1]

Taylor continues: "In every area of the world there is steady pressure against Christianity and continued attempts to abolish 'discrimination' as to creed by making the humanistic creed the standard of all law with respect to religion, the state, and morality. We are in the midst of a world-wide humanistic legal revolution which is even more radical than the bloody revolutions of humanism."[2]

Not only has this new religion of scientific humanism controlled the development of the Russian state and laws (during the U.S.S.R.), but it is also increasingly becoming the foundation for laws in the United States. Thus, in relation to life issues, we see laws being proposed or passed that incorporate this new "humanistic religion." In many diverse ways, the rights of individuals are changing.

Concerning the matter of capital punishment, the basic scientific, humanistic approach is that laws should deter and *cure*. This seems a much more benevolent way to view criminals, that is, essentially as patients to be treated. However, C. S. Lewis had this to say on the subject:

> This doctrine, merciful though it appears really means that each one of us, from the moment he breaks the law, is deprived of the rights of a human being. The reason is this. The humanitarian theory removes from punishment the concept of desert [what the criminal deserves]. But the concept of desert is the only connecting link between punishment and justice. It is only as deserved or undeserved that a sentence can be [seen as] just or unjust. I do not contend that the question "Is it deserved?" is the only one we can reasonably ask about a punishment. We may very properly ask whether it is likely to deter others and to reform the criminal. But neither of these last two questions is a question about justice. There is no sense in talking about a just deterrent or a just cure. We demand of a deterrent not whether it is just, but whether it succeeds. Thus when we only consider what will cure him or deter others, we have tacitly removed him from the sphere of justice altogether; instead of a person, a subject of rights, we now have a mere object, a "case" to be treated in a clinic.[3]

In other words, when criminals are treated as patients, it depersonalizes the criminal and reduces him to someone who has no free will. His crimes were motivated by his illness, and therefore he is not responsible but needs to be "reprogrammed."

Lewis worried about the emergence of a therapeutic never-never land into which criminals vanish overnight into institutions for treatment. I believe we should share this concern.

DISTINGUISHING KILLING FROM MURDER

What does the Bible say about the subject? Does not the Bible say, "Thou shalt not kill" (Exodus 20:13, KJV)? And does not this, therefore, forbid the taking of life in capital punishment? So some people claim. Yet if we examine the Scripture more carefully, we see that this cannot be correct. The Hebrew term used here is *ratsach,* meaning murder. It is used in both places in the Old Testament where the Ten Commandments are given. Whenever the commandments are quoted in the New Testament, every case uses the Greek word *phoneuo,* the verb for committing murder. The commandment is actually meant to read, "You shall not murder."

The Ten Commandments are found in Exodus 20. If the commandment "not to kill" means that we should under no circumstances ever take a life, whether in murder or in capital punishment, we are faced with a tremendous inconsistency. For the very God who tells us in Exodus 20 that we shall not kill, in Exodus 21:12 says, "He who strikes a man so that he dies shall surely be put to death."

Does the same God command us not to kill in one chapter and to kill in the next? In Exodus 21:15 we read, "And he who strikes his father or his mother shall surely be put to death." And again in verse 17, "And he who curses his father or his mother shall surely be put to death." In verses 22 and 23, we read that if a person injures a pregnant woman, he also is to be put to death. In all, Exodus 21 references six specific crimes for which God commands the death penalty. Furthermore, in Deuteronomy 32:39, God says, "I kill and I make alive." If killing in any form were a sin, God Himself would be guilty.

In Genesis 9:6, God makes this statement: "Whoever sheds man's blood, by man his blood shall be shed; for in the image of God He made man." This commandment was given immediately after the flood, when God decided to exercise capital punishment upon virtually the whole earth. Until this point there had been no commandment concerning capital punishment. It is obvious that unless God gives to man the right to take another life, it would be blasphemous on our part to take the lives of others. Yet God is delegating to mankind the responsibility of taking the lives of murderers. This was given to Noah. It is, therefore, for the whole human race and has nothing to do with the Mosaic covenant.

This is all well and good for the Old Testament. Yet did Jesus do away with capital punishment in the New Testament?

Carl F. H. Henry was a well-known writer on Christian personal ethics and a biblical scholar. He pointed out that in the Sermon on the Mount, "Jesus' emphasis on the sixth commandment unveils the inner spiritual attitude of hate as a wicked sin. But to the Old Testament command he does not add that capital punishment and war are wrong. If that is the sense of the commandment, it must belong to the Old Testament conception. But the Old Testament record cannot be reconciled to this alternative."[4]

Jesus's emphasis is the fact that murder may also be committed in the heart, but He is not changing the basic commandment as it is found in the Old Testament, where capital punishment is not only allowed but commanded by God. I believe the testimony of Scripture is clear. God abhors murder. But under certain circumstances, He permits killing if such deaths further the ultimate causes of life and justice.

WHAT ABOUT DETERRENCE?

Does capital punishment discourage other murderers? Dr. Isaac Ehrlich of the University of Chicago is an economic theorist who presented his views on capital punishment before the U.S. Supreme Court. He compiled some impressive data, analyzing it according to modern methods of statistics, and concluded that, from 1933 to 1969, every execution of a murderer may have saved as many as seven or eight lives. He explained this on the basis that all human action is based on some assessment of costs and benefits. A predictable use of capital punishment is—or was—a cost of homicide, and when criminals were aware of this, there was a restraining effect upon the number of homicides committed. Ehrlich's analysis led writer M. Stanton Evans to declare, "Political activists concerned about the sanctity of life should favor, not oppose, the use of capital punishment."[5]

Is Capital Punishment Constitutional?

The Eighth Amendment of the U.S. Constitution prohibits "cruel and unusual punishment."[6] Some modern thinkers want to redefine capital punishment as cruel and unusual punishment. But the Fifth Amendment implies that there is such a thing as the death penalty: "No person shall be held to answer for a capital, or otherwise infamous crime, unless..."[7] The death penalty was used from the colonial era through the founding era up to the present. Not until the 1960s and 1970s did anybody begin to define capital punishment as "cruel and unusual punishment." If the mode of capital punishment is proven to be cruel, then that is to be changed, as has happened from time to time. Thus, we have graduated from firing squads and hangings and the gas chamber to lethal injection in some states.

A Teaching Moment

Did you ever consider what society teaches about the value of human life by either using or not using the death penalty? Dennis Prager, a Jewish conservative commentator and radio talk-show host, observed, "It is a cosmic injustice to allow a murderer to keep his life."[8] In a recent column, he listed ten reasons he favors capital punishment. Here is reason number two: "Killing murderers is society's only way to teach how terrible murder is. The only real way a society can express its revulsion at any criminal behavior is through the punishment it metes out. If murderers all got 10 years in prison and thieves all got 20 years in prison, that would be society's way of saying that thievery is worse than murder. A society that kills murderers is saying that murder is more heinous a crime than a society that keeps all its murderers alive."[9] In the same column, Prager recounts one of the all-too-common tales of a murderer who was released from prison on a legal technicality—only to murder again.[10]

CONCLUSION

How would Jesus want us to vote on the matter of capital punishment? Opponents of capital punishment want us to believe that He would have us oppose the death penalty under any circumstances. And sometimes they aim their arguments at our emotions rather than our minds.

However, I believe the Bible teaches us that there is a place for capital punishment. Of course, there should be every possible safeguard in the exercise of capital punishment in order to protect the falsely accused from being put to death.

Rather than the death penalty denying man's dignity, it upholds it. When human beings deliberately and cold-bloodedly murder other human beings who are made in the image of God, the murderers have forfeited their right to life. Certainly they should be given the chance to repent and make peace with God, but they also should pay for their crimes, even if that means paying with their very lives.

Only by misunderstanding the Bible and destroying the links between Jesus and His Father in the Old Testament could one conclude that Jesus would oppose the death penalty. We should strive to know the Jesus of the Bible (both the Old and the New Testaments) before we cast our ballots on this important issue.

War: Is It Ever Justified?

Blessed are the peacemakers,
for they shall be called sons of God.
—MATTHEW 5:9

It's a subject that has been on the minds and hearts of the American people for some time. Let me say, first and unequivocally, that I hate war. In fact, every right-minded person hates war. War is a great evil. Only tyrants, aggressors, madmen, and the devil love war. Thousands, millions, tens of millions of people have lost their lives in the thunderous inferno that is war.

During one of the many armed conflicts between Great Britain and France, an eighteenth-century British pastor named Samuel Pearce made this comment in a sermon he delivered on a national day of thanksgiving for his country's victories over the French:

> Should any one expect that I shall introduce the *destruction* of our foes, by the late victories gained off the coasts of Egypt and Ireland, as the object of pleasure and gratitude, he will be disappointed. The man who can take pleasure at the destruction of his fellow men, is a cannibal at heart…but to the heart of him who calls himself a disciple of the merciful Jesus, let such pleasure be an everlasting stranger. Since in that sacred volume, which I revere as the fair gift of heaven to man, I am taught, that "of one blood God hath made all nations," [Acts 17:26] it is impossible for me

not to regard every man as my brother, and to consider, that national differences ought not to excite personal animosities.[1]

I am definitely not a materialist or a militarist. On the other hand, I am not a pacifist. Pacifists believe that no war is ever justified. To their way of thinking, there is no "just" war. They would ask, as the late Dr. Gleason Archer observed, "How could a good God, a God of peace, condone warfare?"[2] Indeed, how could Jesus Christ, the Prince of Peace, condone warfare? Yet, as Archer noted, the Bible, in referring to such wars as that of Reuben, Gad, and Manasseh against the pagan tribes of the Transjordan, states: "For many fell dead, because the war was God's" (1 Chronicles 5:22). That concept is repeated many times throughout the Old Testament.

Though it is certainly a critical issue, attitudes about war are divisive. Well-meaning professing Christians are deeply divided on this point, so it is an issue well worth exploring here.

WHAT DOES THE BIBLE SAY?

Nowhere does the Bible say that war is justified. However, it never says it is not justified, either. It does not deal specifically with the issue, but there are a great many instances from which we can draw definite conclusions.

Genesis 14:8–20 describes the first "just" war. In fact, it grows out of the first war in all of recorded history—about two thousand years before Julius Caesar conquered Gaul, about seventeen hundred years before Alexander led his phalanxes from Macedonia to Persia, and about one thousand years before a wooden horse was pulled through the gates of Troy during the Trojan War.

The first war in all of recorded history took place two thousand years before Christ was born, the result of some very interesting events—especially in light of where we are now. In Genesis 14, we read that Amraphel, the king of Shinar, together with three confederates, including Chedorlaomer, invaded Canaan—particularly the land of the plain around the Dead Sea. He attacked a number of cities, including Sodom and Gomorrah.

I think that is fascinating. I am sure most of you reading that Amraphel was the king of Shinar would have thought little about it. However, if you go back to Genesis 11:2, you will find that men built the Tower of Babel in the land of Shinar; today we call that region Mesopotamia, or Iraq. Chedorlaomer may very well have been the king of Babylon; the city lies but thirty miles south of Baghdad.

Actually, we have come full circle: the very first war involved the invasion of Israel by the king of Shinar; today we are involved in a war in that very same area. But those early kings made one mistake (aggressors always seem to make fatal mistakes): they took Lot and his family captive, and one of Lot's servants managed to escape. The servant ran back to Abram (or Abraham) and told him what had happened.

Abraham didn't respond as many people in those circumstances might have. Rather than holding Lot accountable for his own choice to set his tent toward Sodom, he immediately armed his 318 servants (which indicates a household staff of more than 1,000, including women and children) and started out on a forced march. They overcame the kings in confederacy with Amraphel somewhere in Dan, in the northern area of Israel.

We then read that Abraham divided his forces in two, and at night they attacked the aggressors from opposite directions. Abraham's trust was in the Lord, and he was awarded a great victory. Though considerably outnumbered, he set the enemy into a panic, and they fled for their lives. Abraham's forces chased them north of Damascus, and Abraham recovered all the prisoners and their goods.

So he returned with Lot and his family. But as he was passing by Jerusalem, he was met by Melchizedek, whose name means the "king of righteousness." Melchizedek was, in fact, the king of Salem. (Salem is the ancient name for Jerusalem. It is the same word we know today as *shalom*, thus his name meant the "king of peace.") "The king of righteousness and peace" meets Abraham and blesses him for his great and righteous victory in vanquishing the aggressors and restoring justice.

In the New Testament book of Hebrews, we are told a number of times that Melchizedek is a type of Christ. Interestingly, we read this statement in Genesis: "Then Melchizedek king of Salem brought out bread and wine; he was the priest of God Most High" (14:18). Of course, Jesus is our high priest, and He used bread and wine as the representatives of His broken body and shed blood for us. Abraham's return from victorious battle is blessed by this priest of God Most High, a type of our Lord, the "Prince of Peace," who is here represented by the king of peace. I think that is quite significant.

We might think that a man like Abraham, who was known for his piety and godliness, would not be likely to engage in warfare or, if he were engaged, would not be successful. But Abraham's piety did not prevent his military prowess. In fact, it undergirded and strengthened him in the task.

Abraham used tactics that have been repeated over and over through the centuries, most recently by the allied forces in the first and second Gulf wars. This did not take place during the theocracy from Moses's time; this was five hundred years earlier. Abraham was not commanded by God to wage this war; it was left to his own conscience and his beliefs about right and wrong. It was not his personal household or his property that had been taken. But to release captives and restore property, Abraham put his own life in jeopardy, acted in faith, and won a decisive victory.

There is no doubt, Melchizedek's blessing on Abraham was God's blessing. Throughout the Old Testament there are numerable instances of just wars. Though it is true we are to avoid all acts of personal violence, author Robert Morey noted, "The use of force to overthrow tyranny is blessed and sanctioned by God Himself. People have the moral obligation to take whatever action is necessary to fight for the freedom and liberty of all the oppressed peoples of the world."[3]

WHAT OF THE NEW TESTAMENT?

Once again the Old Testament is instructive, but doesn't Jesus, the Prince of Peace, change all of that? Didn't He tell us to be peacemakers? Didn't He tell us we should resist evil? Absolutely. He did. Unfortunately, there are many people who do not follow what He taught and twist and distort it to the oppression and destruction of others. These statements found in the Sermon on the Mount are part of His teaching regarding personal ethics. They are not instructions on how nations are to govern or approach international relationships. His words are to individuals, and they are based upon the standards of a Christian's personal ethics.

How do we see this? Jesus said, "But I tell you not to resist an evil person. But whoever slaps you on your right cheek, turn the other to him also" (Matthew 5:39). What does He mean? For you, dear parent, if you're at home with your children, and a man breaks into your home and stabs one of them, are you to hold out the other child so he can take a slash at her? Is that what it means to turn the other cheek? Or if a neighbor is mugged, beaten, and left for dead, should you apprehend the mugger to bring him back so he can take a crack at her other cheek. What would you think?

What about the bank president who reads that Jesus said, "Give to him who asks you, and from him who wants to borrow from you do not turn away" (Matthew 5:42)? Should he lend whatever amount is asked by anyone who applies for a loan? Would that work?

Why do these things not follow? Did not Jesus say these words? Yes, but Jesus is talking about *personal Christian ethics*. (We touched on this in chapter 5.) You see, it is not *my* little girl I'm telling you to hold up to be slashed. It is not *your* cheek that your neighbor is turning to be smitten. It is not the bank president's money that he is giving away. It is our own cheeks we are to turn. It is our own monies we are to lend.

Jesus also said that we are to "resist not evil" (Matthew 5:39, KJV). Is that what an entire nation is to do? Are police forces and armies unnecessary? If we would find out what nations are to do, look at Romans 13, where teachings about the magistrate and about civil power are given, wherein we are told to obey the government: "Let every soul be subject to the governing authorities. For there is no authority except from God, and the authorities that exist are appointed by God.... For rulers are not a terror to good works, but to evil" (Romans 13:1, 3). And consider 1 Peter 2:13, 15–17: "Therefore submit yourselves to every ordinance of man for the Lord's sake.... For this is the will of God, that by doing good you may put to silence the ignorance of foolish men—as free, yet not using liberty as a cloak for vice, but as bond-servants of God. Honor all people. Love the brotherhood. Fear God. Honor the king."

The entire basis of how nations are to conduct themselves is justice. The magistrate bears not the sword (the symbol of punishment and even death) in vain.

There are many other things Jesus said that make it very clear He was not a pacifist. We are, in our personal lives, to be peacemakers. We are to live, as much as we can, at peace with everyone. The Bible teaches this very clearly.

While Abraham was a successful warrior, he also was a peacemaker. In Genesis 13, we read that fighting broke out between his servants and Lot's servants. It was Abraham who made peace and said, in effect, to his nephew, "Brother, we should not have such fighting among us. So you take your people and choose whichever way you want to go, that there may be peace."

A little later we see that Abraham signed the first peace treaty in history with the Philistines, and this accord lasted for several generations, because he was a man of peace. He nevertheless knew there were times when a person has to pick up arms.

Some of the other teachings of Jesus show this distinction even more clearly. In a parable He spoke with obvious approval of a king who waged a just war to punish wicked people by putting them to death (Luke 19:12–27). In Luke 6, when dealing with Roman and Jewish soldiers, Jesus never told them to leave the military or that it was morally wrong to be soldiers. In fact, when talking to a centurion, Jesus said, "I say to you, I have not found such great faith, not even in Israel!" (Luke 7:9). He did not tell the centurion that, if he had such faith, the first thing he ought to do was resign from the military. There are other instances of centurions who demonstrated that kind of faith, and they were never told to leave the military.

Furthermore, neither Jesus nor any of the apostles ever said that Rome should disband its armies or that there should be no police. Never is such a thing found in the Bible. Jesus clearly taught that wars would continue until the end of time. One of the signs of the end times, we are told, is that there shall be wars and rumors of war (see Mark 13:7). In fact, there will be a great war at the very end.

In talking about such things, Jesus very well could have said to His disciples, "This is what ordinarily would happen, but you must do everything in your power to prevent that from coming to pass. You must go on the march to bring about pacifism in the world."

Jesus said in John 18:36 that if His church were an earthly kingdom, it would be perfectly proper for His disciples to take up arms and fight for Him. But His kingdom is not earthly; it is spiritual. By the way, the church is not to initiate war. When it attempted to do so in the Middle Ages, it was wrong. It remains for the civil government to have that authority—and only the civil authorities.

In His parables, Jesus over and over again pictured rulers as using valid force to punish wrongdoers. (See, for example, Matthew 18:21–35 and Mark 12:9.) There are those who say we should only resist evil passively, but Jesus was not one of them. At the beginning and the end of His ministry, Jesus used force to cleanse the temple. He made a whip out of cords, and the moneychangers felt that whip on their backs as He overturned their tables and drove them out of the temple. They were terrified of Him. Throughout His ministry Jesus talked about God's use of force on the Day of Judgment to punish rebellious sinners.

WHAT OF PASSIVE RESISTANCE?

Mohandas Gandhi claimed passive resistance as the way to respond to evil. What many fail to understand is that the only reason it worked was that he used it against the British Empire, which after the Victorian era was more imbued with the principles of Christ than any nation in the world. British tanks were not willing to roll over passive Hindus sitting in the streets.

But had Gandhi been up against Josef Stalin or Adolf Hitler, we would have seen a radically different outcome. Whenever passive resistance has been used against such tyrants, it has been met with destruction and bloodshed; consider Hungary in 1956, Poland in 1980, and Tiananmen Square in 1989, to name a few. Such ungodly aggressors have massacred innocent people without a shred of conscience. Passive resistance does not work with such people, and Christ, knowing the hearts of men, knew that full well.

WHAT OF JUST WARS?

What is a just war? Throughout its history the Christian church has maintained that there was and is such a thing as a just war as well as an unjust war. In fact, down through the history of the church, the greatest of its theologians and reformers have held this to be true. Augustine, the greatest mind in the first thousand years after Paul; Thomas Aquinas, the greatest theologian of the Catholic Church; Martin Luther, John Calvin, John Knox, and other Reformers down to our day—all have held that there is such a thing as a just war. So what is it?

★ It is *defensive in nature;* it is for the purpose of protecting the lives and liberty of those who have been plundered, attacked, or treated unjustly.

★ It is *waged by a legitimate government* and not individuals. We are told over and over in the Bible that we are not to practice personal vengeance. The Bible says, "Vengeance is Mine, I will repay" (Romans 12:19).

★ The purpose of a just war is to *establish permanent peace* and not personal aggrandizement. Consider the story of Abraham. He refused to take anything that belonged to his aggressors.

There are a number of other qualities of a just war. One of them, of course, is that every effort be made to establish peace beforehand. Yet when attempts at peace fail, the just war concept is clearly seen in the Scriptures.

We should remember, however, that there have been others besides sincere Christians who are interested in pacifism. I believe many Christians sincerely believe that God would have them to be pacifists. I do not for one moment doubt that fact, and I commend them for standing up for their principles and doing what they believe to be right. I think they are in error, but I commend them for their faithfulness. However, there are others who are not Christians and who do not have sincere motives, but for insincere reasons and malevolent intent, they have engaged in peace or pacifist movements.

During most of my life, the threat of communism hung over all of life. It was always there, always present. Only when a hard-line president, Ronald Reagan, came along and acknowledged the depth of the threat was there a major change in that threat. Thankfully, the Soviet Union essentially imploded, thanks to the policies of Reagan in tandem with Pope John Paul II. Both of them aided the resistance in Poland, which eventually led, like dominos, to the failure of communism in most of its strongholds. Writing for Charles Colson's ministry, Leslie Carbone noted, "The Evil Empire crumbled because President Reagan's defense buildup forced them to keep up; because communism stifles prosperity, they couldn't maintain the same pace that America could."[4]

Meanwhile, today's dominant media culture reports all that is going wrong in the war in Iraq with barely a word about any significant progress being made there. Sometimes our media coverage seems to be coming solely from the *Al Jazeera* perspective.

What is critical to remember is that the goal for the war in Iraq that began in 2003 is not just winning the war; it is about winning the peace.

WAR IS A GREAT EVIL, BUT NOT THE ONLY EVIL

War is a great evil. It is a tragic thing. All Christians should abhor it and do what they can to prevent it. We are to live at peace with all others, as much as the possibility lies within us. However, there are times when we *must* fight. So have the greatest of Christian theologians and Reformers down through the centuries believed, and so the founders of this nation believed as well. The war that overthrew the tyranny of Great Britain, the war that gave us our independence and our freedom, was a war many Americans trembled before. But there were those who were not afraid.

Contrast Bertrand Russell's attitude on war—war is so evil we should do anything, including surrender, rather than go to war—with the attitude of Patrick Henry. Russell, an atheist, wrote a book entitled *Why I Am Not a Christian.* On the other hand, Henry was a Christian. For Russell, the loss of this life was a loss of everything and therefore should be avoided at any cost— "peace at any price." Henry believed that the loss of this life was but the initiation of another everlasting and undying life with Christ in paradise.

It was that faith that strengthened Patrick Henry for the conflict, the same faith that strengthened Abraham for his conflict. It is the same faith that has strengthened millions of others in this country and in other parts of the world to overcome the evil of tyranny, even at the cost of their lives.

It was Patrick Henry who believed and expressed that belief in these familiar words: "Is life so dear or peace so sweet as to be purchased at the price of chains and slavery?"

"Yes," said Bertrand Russell.

'No," said Patrick Henry. "Forbid it, Almighty God. I know not what course others may take, but as for me, give me liberty, or give me death."[5]

I thank God for the faith that steels the nerves of people and gives iron to their backbone and enables them to stand up against the tyrants of this world. Without faith and strength, there would be no liberty anywhere on the earth today. It exists thanks to the sacrifice of people who believed in that One who is the Resurrection and the Life, who has promised that those who trust in Him shall never truly die. I pray that God would grant us that faith in this country again. I pray that God would restore to us that strength of conviction. I pray for that faith in the living God that, though we may do all in our power to maintain peace at home and throughout the world, when critical moments come, we shall not cringe and hide. I pray that we shall stand for that which we believe, even as Abraham stood for what he believed, even at the venture of his own life. Jesus is the captain in this well-fought fight.

THE MEDIEVAL MISTAKE

During the Middle Ages, the Catholic Church made what I called earlier "the medieval mistake." They used the sword to enforce their understanding of Christian doctrine. Jesus never intended that we use arms to enforce His doctrines. Reformer Martin Luther said, "I will preach, speak, write the truth, but will force it on no one, for faith must be accepted willingly, and without compulsion."[6] Regarding those who light the sticks to burn heretics at the stake, he added, "If fire is the right cure for heresy, then the fagot-burners are the most learned doctors on earth; nor need we study any more; he that has brute force on his side may burn his adversary at the stake."[7]

Truth is the cornerstone of Christianity. Jesus calls the Holy Spirit the Spirit of truth, and when Jesus prayed for unity within the church, He prayed, "Sanctify them by Your truth. Your word is truth" (John 17:17).

Christians are sanctified by the truth, and if we abide by Jesus's teaching, the truth shall set us free (see John 8:32). Thus, the sword of human action has no power to unify or protect the true church.

Religious differences are not to be solved by the sword. Instead, declared Puritan leader (and dissident from fellow Puritans) Roger Williams, founder of Rhode Island: "[Religious differences] are only to be fought against with that sword which is only (in soul matters) able to conquer, to wit, the sword of God's spirit, the Word of God."[8] Williams reminded his Christian brethren who desired the purity of New Testament Christianity that another facet they needed to claim was that we serve the Prince of Peace. Those who live by the sword shall die by the sword.

Throughout the centuries, Christians made this mistake repeatedly. I believe that in America today, for the most part, we have corrected this error. While some fringe groups may claim to be Christian and advocate violence to promote their agenda, by and large the church of Jesus Christ does not advocate violence to promote purity of doctrine. The church no longer burns heretics at the stake. Conflicts between Catholics and Protestants are fought through discussion, not force.[9]

THE ISLAMIC THREAT

The cold war is over, thanks be to God. However, in our day there is an ongoing war on terror—or more accurately—a war against radical Islam. Like the communists before them, the jihadists want to take over the world. They will not rest until they blow up the White House or fly the black flag over it. Bill O'Reilly, host of the popular Fox News show *The O'Reilly Factor* and a syndicated columnist, noted, "America will sooner or later have to defeat the Muslims who hate us, or be subjected to continuous terror and violence. If you think I am overstating things, consider this: Our so-called friends, the Saudis, are paying the families of suicide bombers thousands of dollars for their 'sacrifice.'"[10]

A few Muslim doctrines make it difficult to come to terms with the jihadists. First, there is the concept of *hudna*. This allows a Muslim leader to make a treaty with non-Muslims with no intention of keeping it! The treaty is temporary, and when convenient and expedient for the jihadists, they will break it.

Another doctrine is *waqf*, which means that once a territory is Islamic, it is forever Islamic, even if the unbelievers temporarily regain it. Have you ever wondered why the Islamic world will not let Israel live in peace? Consider a small matchbox on a football field. The matchbox represents Israel; the football field represents its Arab neighbors. Despite their immense holdings, the Arab world cannot allow Israel to exist in peace. The doctrine of *waqf* helps us understand. At a Camp David meeting coordinated by President Bill Clinton, even though Israeli prime minister Ehud Barak offered Yasser Arafat 98 percent of what Arafat wanted, the terrorist leader turned it down. The Arab world will not rest until Israel is destroyed. Why? Because of waqf. Every day that Israel exists, Islamic doctrine is undermined.

A third consideration about dealing with Islam is the love of death that is so prevalent in Muslim doctrine. When we were dealing with the Soviet Union, at least they had a fear of death and a desire to live; hence, the doctrine of MAD (Mutually Assured Destruction) kept the Soviets from initiating a nuclear war. If jihadists acquire a nuclear weapon, they will have no such compunction. They look forward to dying for Allah so they can receive their promised seventy-two virgins in paradise.

CONCLUSION

How would Jesus vote in regard to war? He certainly would view military force as a last resort. I realize that some sincere, committed Christians disagree about this. For example, I believe the Amish are sincere Christians. Look at the incredibly kind and merciful way they dealt with a horrible murder by an outsider in their own community in 2006 and the love they showed the murderer's family. It was a strong witness to the love of Christ. Now, that being said, the Amish will not pick up the sword under any circumstances, even for self-defense. I can understand that. However, would it not be accurate to say that the freedom the Amish enjoy is at the expense of those who do bear arms when their country calls them? We could all be speaking German today, or Japanese, if not enough Americans had enlisted to fight for our country in World Wars I and II.

George Washington, our nation's first commander in chief, respected the Quakers of Pennsylvania and their pacifist ways. However, he understood that their freedom to practice their religion without interference came about because other colonists picked up their arms to fight for the American cause.

In short, I think Jesus would, on occasion, have us vote in such a way that supports a just war. Where we draw the line between just wars and unjust wars, good Christians and people of goodwill may disagree, but there is a legitimate time to fight for one's country.

Education and Our Schools

And these words which I command you today
shall be in your heart.
You shall teach them diligently to your children,
and shall talk of them when you sit in your house,
when you walk by the way, when you lie down,
and when you rise up.

—DEUTERONOMY 6:6–7

A critical issue of importance in each election cycle is education. There are huge differences in this field between those with a Christian world-and-life view and those without such a view.

In a political cartoon, little Johnny is eight years old. He is standing on a street corner with tears streaming down his cheeks. A yellow school bus with an open door waits impatiently for him to board, and he obviously does not want to do so. His mother bends over him pleading, "But, Johnny, sweetheart, Mother and Daddy want you to learn how to read and write and do arithmetic."

He responds, "So then why are you sending me back to school?"

For the first two hundred years of this nation's history, education was explicitly Christian, and it produced amazing results. In the late 1700s, John Adams observed that to find an illiterate man in New England was as rare as a comet.[1] How interesting that with the rise of secularism in our educational institutions has come a sharp rise in illiteracy. While more than a trillion dollars has been poured *into* the secular public-education system in America and Christ has been taken *out* of it, the illiteracy rate has increased thirty-two times. Our literacy rate is rapidly plunging to that of Zambia. What a contrast to the era of the Founding Fathers, where education was Christian and literacy widespread.

Stunning. The U.S. Department of Education, which has every reason *not* to reveal how bad the situation is, says that more than ninety million Americans lack simple literacy.[2] Unbelievable, is it not?

I saw another political cartoon showing two college graduates walking down the aisle after the commencement exercises, wearing mortarboards and robes and carrying their college diplomas in their hands. One turns to the other on the way out and says, "Well, did you learn anything?"

This problem began in the last half of the twentieth century, when schools became more concerned about socialization than basic learning. One education historian discovered by comparing a great many scores over a great many years that American education had lost, on average, almost one year of academic achievement per decade throughout the twentieth century. Think about what that means. If you have a college diploma, you have about the same education a sixth grader had in the first decade of the twentieth century. Some might say that's nonsense, but read a sampling of questions asked of sixth graders in 1905.

★ "The orthography quiz asked us to spell twenty words, including *elucidation* and *animosity.*"

★ "An arithmetic question asked us to find the interest on an 8 percent note for nine hundred dollars running two years, two months, and six days."

★ "In reading we were required…to give the meanings of words such as panegyric and eyrie [sometimes spelled *aerie*]."

★ "Among geography's ten questions was, 'Name two countries producing large quantities of wheat, two of cotton, two of coal.'"

★ "In history we were to name the principal political questions which have been advocated since the Civil War and the party which advocated each."[3]

Somebody asked me, "Well, aren't all other countries going through the same thing?" No, they are not. In comparative examinations with the seventeen leading industrialized nations of the world, the United States came out last in two categories and first in none.

There is an irony to all this as well. Not only do American students not do as well as those of other nations, but because of the push for "self-esteem" education, our students *believe* they are doing better than they are. For example, columnist Thomas Sowell cited one international test of thirteen-year-olds in which Korean children ranked first in math and Americans ranked last. Sixty-eight percent of American children believed they were "good at mathematics" compared to only 23 percent of the Korean students.[4] Thus the American youngsters ranked first in self-esteem and last in actual skills.

Here is how our students are actually doing:

★ 95% of college students could not find Vietnam on a map.

★ 45% of high schoolers in Baltimore could not find the United States on a world map.

★ Many college students in North Carolina said Russia was somewhere near the Panama Canal.[5]

Al Shanker, president of the American Federation of Teachers, noted that "only 6 percent of high school seniors can read a newspaper editorial, write a two-page essay and complete a two-step math problem."[6]

One survey of schools in France, Germany, and Japan showed that U.S. high-school students received half as many hours in the core curriculum studies as students in those countries.[7] However, we do learn our new ABCs. One political cartoon showed a father looking down at a little boy who is looking at a paper. The father says, "New Math I've heard of, but what are the new ABC's?" Very quickly the little boy recites them: "AIDS, birth control, and condoms. Don't you know anything, Dad?"

No, I am afraid our educational system is in a catastrophic decline.

AN ALIEN AND HOSTILE FORCE

You may recall that a blue-ribbon panel was appointed by President Ronald Reagan in the mid-1980s to examine our education failures. The panel concluded American education was so bad that if a foreign power had done to our public schools what the public schools have done to themselves, it would be considered an act of war. We would send in the marines to battle such an alien and hostile force. And, my friend, this is exactly who has done it to our schools; the bureaucrats, the union leaders, the National Education Association (NEA), for the most part, have indeed virtually destroyed the once-great public-education system in America.

One woman, having been out of teaching for about fifteen years, returned and was startled to discover that the phonics system had been replaced with the look-say method, which is nothing more than pictures and guessing. It is a system that has produced tens of millions of functional illiterates, according to the Department of Education.

The teacher also found her students' work in history to be very disappointing. Every lesson seemed to denigrate democracy, capitalism, and even Western civilization. I do not believe even one of the fifty major universities in this country teaches a course in Western civilization anymore. New Age is in. Aztec culture is in. But Western civilization, which is denigrated as merely the writings of dead, white, male Europeans, is most decidedly out.

Our students are unfamiliar with the values that have made America great—starting with its Christian foundations and its belief in God. Paul

Blanshard, one of the leading humanist educators of the twentieth century, said, "Our schools may not teach Johnny to read properly, but the fact that Johnny is in school until he is sixteen tends to lead toward the elimination of religious superstition [with which he entered school]."[8] That religious superstition, in case you do not know, is what we call Christianity.

Several years ago one of our ministry vice presidents related to me that his next-door neighbor sent his five-year-old son to kindergarten for his first day of school. When the boy came home from kindergarten, his mother asked him, "So, honey, what did you learn in your first day of kindergarten?"

He answered, "You can't even prove that Jesus Christ ever lived."

That was the first day. Exactly what the teacher actually said is not known, but that was the take-home message for the little boy. I thought, *Wow, they don't waste any time.* Not only is the educational accomplishment of our schools disastrous, but what it has done to our students morally is even worse. In 1955 a textbook on journalism made this interesting comment: "While crime news must be published, it should be balanced with the reporting of positive events. School news, for example, is almost always [positive] good news." That was 1955.

Look at some school news that made the newspapers:

★ "High-school girls active in prostitution ring."
★ "Scanners installed to deter guns brought to school." (Reportedly, 130,000 guns are brought to school every morning in America.)
★ "Student dead after shots ring out in stadium."
★ "Broward schools fight sexual harassment."
★ "Student who wanted an 'A' fatally stabs teacher."
★ "SAT scores hit all-time low."

★ "Pupils held hostage by knife-wielder."

★ "Drug pusher arrested on high-school campus."

★ "Condoms distributed to seventh graders."

On and on it goes. We have forgotten the words of George Washington, who had nothing vaguely resembling the kind of "refined" education many are getting today when he said, "Whatever may be conceded to the influence of refined education on minds of peculiar structure, reason and experience both forbid us to expect that national morality can prevail in exclusion of religious principle."[9]

We cannot get rid of religious principle. The founders of this country never intended that religion should be stricken from our schools. The first Congress of the United States passed the Northwest Ordinance, which said, "Religion, morality, and knowledge being necessary for good government, schools and the means of education shall forever be encouraged."[10] Schools? Yes. For what? Religion, number one. Morality, number two. Knowledge, number three.

We got rid of religion, then we got rid of morality, and now we are losing ground on knowledge. We may be dumb Americans, but we feel good about ourselves.

What we hear from the school unions is that they need more money. Next time you hear that, just remember that we spend more money per student than any other nation in the world. The problem is not money; the problem is the philosophy. We have brought about a moral educational collapse equivalent to an attack by a hostile foreign power.

You may remember *McGuffey's Readers,* which were first published in 1836 and sold more than 122 million copies. The series was thoroughly Christian. It was later expurgated of its Christian content, but this is what William H. McGuffey, a Presbyterian clergyman and an educator, wrote in

1854: "If you can induce a community to doubt the genuineness and authenticity of the Scriptures; to question the reality and obligations of religion; to hesitate, undeciding, whether there is any such thing as virtue or vice; whether there be an eternal state of retribution beyond the grave; or whether there exists any such being as God, you have broken down the barriers of moral virtue and hoisted the floodgates of immorality and crime."[11] Can you imagine a better description of what we are witnessing in this country today?

All education was in the hands of the church and the clergy until 1830. Horace Mann, the founder of public education, stated that he wanted to get education out of the hands of the church—essentially, to take away the Christian element.[12] (This secularization was fulfilled a century later.)

A more modern commentator, Barbara Walters, once gave a report, saying, "The alarm has sounded. The clock is ticking. But most of us are still asleep." What was she referring to? The nuclear threat? Global warming? The AIDS epidemic?

No, she was referring to the deterioration of American education. Most high-school students she surveyed thought the Holocaust was a Jewish holiday. But the real crisis, Walters argued, was one of character. "Today's high school seniors live in a world of misplaced values," she said. They have no sense of discipline. No goals. They care only for themselves. In short, they are "becoming a generation of undisciplined cultural barbarians."[13]

Many adults do not realize what has happened in the schools since they graduated twenty-five, thirty-five, or forty some years ago. It is a different world today. Our schools could be changed by a president with the courage to appoint a secretary of education who could clean up the system and reestablish the education of character. In the meantime, Christian schools and homeschooling are picking up the slack. I thank the Lord for that. Let me also say I thank God for all the Christians continuing to teach in an increasingly difficult public-school system. We need Christians in public schools teaching, supervising, and overseeing our children.

However, I would advise that you consider your decision carefully before you put your children in an ungodly situation, with teachers who would promote worldly agendas. Not only will your children *not* get a good education, but their beliefs could be dealt a devastating blow at the hands of a secular education system that is the norm in this country today.

THE PURPOSE OF EDUCATION

Read various books in the field of modern education, and you will see a number of different purposes set forth for education. For example, a common one is that we are endeavoring in our educational system to turn out *good citizens* who will take their rightful places in a free democracy. On the surface, this is a noble goal, and many people believe that it is very sound. Yet on closer examination, one finds this is not at all the biblical concept of the purpose for education.

This idea has been held in many forms for a great many centuries, all the way back to the Greek philosophers. They held that the purpose of education was to enable students to become good citizens of the Greek city-states. The purpose of education was ultimately for the benefit of the state. However, this same idea prevails in all totalitarian governments, whether they be Nazi, fascist, or communist. Obviously, this is not the view of education from a Christian perspective.

There are others who say that the purpose of education is self-actualization, namely, the realization of the potential that lies within individual students. As far as it goes, this too holds an element of truth. Yet the theory does not go far enough. The word *education* comes from two Latin words that mean "to lead out" or "to bring out" of the student the potential that is there. The problem is that it does not answer the ultimate question: for what purpose am I going to bring out these latent potentialities? Self-actualization, if it has no further goal, is vanity. Students may be endowed with musical talent, but unless they apply that talent to some higher purpose, it is incomplete. Whether for vain display, for the plaudits of people, or for purely monetary reasons, all of these fall short of the Christian ideal.

This view of education is based on the idea that there is no soul, nothing that exists that is not "matter in motion." Yet to ignore the spiritual realm is to ignore the most important part of our existence.

I heard a talk show as I was driving home for lunch one day. They were discussing sex, particularly extramarital sexual relations. All sorts of people were calling in with advice, suggestions, and thoughts on the matter. Never had I called one of these programs, but by the time I got home, I was so furious that I decided to call in and say my piece. I called and started to say that, in consideration of all things that had to do with this, we needed to consider what God says about sex.

"Wait a minute. Stop right there. We are only considering this from a scientific point of view," was the reply.

I was not going to be cut off quite that easily, and I proceeded to explain to the show host that she had a false concept of knowledge. She was adopting the position of the logical positivist, who says the only way we know anything is empirically and experientially. She was denying, a priori, any possibility of a revelation from God dealing with this matter. Though she tried three or four times to stop me, I was determined not to be stopped, and I spoke my mind for all to hear.

The interesting thing is the presupposition behind this. The radio host was actually shocked at the intrusion of God into "our world." *Who does*

God think He is? You would think He had made the world or something. Her basis was the naturalistic presupposition that there is nothing in the world but humans and nature. Therefore, only these aspects of the question were to be considered. This type of assumption underlies most of our secular education today, so it is obvious that those who adjust to this kind of environment will be maladjusted to God. I warn you that any secular educator employing the popular life-adjustment theories of our time will succeed in totally maladjusting your child to God.

Reformer John Calvin advocated that the purpose of education was that people might know God and glorify Him as God—that in our vocation and in our life, we might know God. Therefore, what is to be the content of our education? Realizing the source of all truth, Calvin saw that we should first study that truth as it is revealed in the Scriptures, which provides us with the proper spectacles to understand what is revealed in God's second book—nature.

Both in the world of nature and in the world of Scripture, we are to find out more about God so that we may love Him, trust Him, exalt Him, and glorify Him. Thus we bring out our potentiality to use for the greater glory of God. We adjust to our environment, our *entire* environment, including that most important part in which we live and move and have our being.

ANTI-CHRISTIAN PROPAGANDA?

Day by day our Judeo-Christian heritage has been a stripped away in the schools so that children today do not learn our true history, for example, the Declaration of Independence. They may or may not learn about our Founding Fathers, and if they do, they learn the myth that they were all deists.[14] Many learn about Martin Luther King Jr. but not the Reverend

Martin Luther King Jr. and the fact that he was a Baptist minister who launched his antiracist crusade from the Southern Christian Leadership Conference, which he organized.

The stories of discrimination against anything Christian in the public schools are legion. In November 2004 in Cupertino, California, a suburb of San Francisco, fifth-grade teacher Stephen Williams was barred by his school district from giving handouts to his students that included excerpts from the Declaration of Independence as well as writings of such historic figures as George Washington, John Adams, and William Penn, because those documents mentioned God. Furthermore, Williams was required to submit all of his lesson plans in advance to the school principal—a standard he says was not applied to any other teacher.[15]

The great A. A. Hodge—professor of systematic theology at Princeton Seminary (in the 1880s, when public schools had not yet spread to every state in the nation) and one of the greatest theologians America has ever seen—made this eagle-eyed prediction when he said "a comprehensive and centralized system of national education, separated from religion,…will prove the most appalling engineer for the propagation of anti-Christian and atheistic unbelief…which this sin-rent world has ever seen."[16]

John Dewey, the father of modern progressive education, so lionized today, started the movement that divorced God from education. He was also one of the signers of *The Humanist Manifesto,* written in the 1930s and rewritten in 1973, which states, "We believe, however, that traditional dogmatic or authoritarian religions that place revelation, God, ritual, or creed above human needs and experience do a disservice to the human species."[17] It also includes this statement: "No deity will save us; we must save ourselves."[18] Such statements could just as easily have come out of the mouths of Karl Marx or Adolf Hitler. And yet those statements are essentially the basis for the state of modern public education.

Professor Jacques Barzun, an eminent educator and author, said in the *New York Review of Books,* "The once proud and efficient public school system [of the United States] has turned into a wasteland where violence and vice share the time with ignorance and idleness."[19] The result: we have tens of millions of illiterates in America who have been turned out by these schools. It is not only unsafe for the students; we have also seen how unsafe it is for the educators.

AN ESSENTIAL MISSING INGREDIENT

In one sense, public education can never succeed, even if the schools tried to be fair to Christian ideals (and some do try). There is one fact that cannot be changed: "The fear of the LORD is the *beginning* of knowledge" (Proverbs 1:7). It is first base. If fear of the Lord is missing, education will fall flat on its face.

Even in my own life, I can see this. I was a bit of a C student and then a college dropout. After I was saved and called to the ministry, I had to return to my undergraduate studies, and I began to get virtually all A's. Why? Because I got smarter? No. Because I was spiritually motivated. A sense of internal motivation can work for a nonbeliever too, but in those who become sanctified, it is like a light bulb clicking on.

CONCLUSION

So how would Jesus vote when it comes to education? Since it is His will that we train our children to love and to fear Him and to love our neighbors as ourselves, I believe He would have us vote in ways that would promote a godly education for our children. We cannot impose a godly education on the ungodly, but at least we can teach our own children in that vein.

As long as God continues to be barred from our public schools, the public-education system will continue to falter. I cannot picture Jesus Christ putting His stamp of approval on our current public-education system—not unless we see a serious overhaul. Ultimately, I think the fairest outcome would allow more freedom for all. The time should end for Christians being taxed twice because they do not want to send their children to learn in public schools. Not everyone can afford a Christian education, and not everyone is able to teach their children at home, but as parents, we will be accountable to God for the education of our children. Therefore, it is up to us to make sure our children are taught well, including being taught to fear the Lord.

8

Economic Concerns

He who is greatest among you
shall be your servant.

—Matthew 23:11

How would Jesus have us vote when it comes to Social Security? How about tax reform?

Foreign trade policy?

Or health care?

These are good questions, and not all of them have right or wrong answers. However, we can glean some guiding principles from the Word of God.

THE IMPACT OF ECONOMICS ON ALL OF LIFE

Economics may seem like an academic and theoretical subject, but it is actually quite practical. Whether we recognize it or not, each of us is enmeshed in the world of economics. So how would Jesus have us vote on economic issues? I think He would want us to be as wise as serpents and as innocent as doves (see Matthew 10:16). I think He would want us to be discerning enough to see through the rhetoric and the crass (but sometimes subtle) attempts of politicians to bankrupt the national treasury in order to buy votes. I believe He would have the church take care of the poor through voluntary means, not through the involuntary means of the government.

Preliminary Answers

Let's delve into a Christian view of economics beyond the political rhetoric and look at some specific economic issues mentioned in the Bible.

How would Jesus have us vote when it comes to Social Security? The Bible tells us to save and plan for the future; for example, "The plans of the diligent lead to profit" (Proverbs 21:5, NIV). But does that mean the government should muscle its way into the savings business, especially when the rate of return on average is much worse than one could receive in the private sector? I always chuckle when I think of the C in FICA—Social Security; the C stands for *contributions* (Federal Insurance Contributions Act), which implies voluntary giving. But if you chose to withhold your contribution, you would be in trouble with the Internal Revenue Service (IRS). Meanwhile, the number of workers per retiree is shrinking. This means that fewer and fewer productive citizens can be taxed to pay for more and more retirees. We have slaughtered some forty million to fifty million potential workers through abortion, and now we are reaping one of the consequences. Any honest attempt to fix Social Security for the future seems to be futile and only hurts the one trying to help (as it did George W. Bush in 2005).

How would Jesus have us vote when it comes to tax reform? I believe He would want us to be more fair than we have been. This question is so important that we will explore it throughout this chapter.

How would Jesus have us vote when it comes to foreign trade? Well-meaning Christians can be found on different sides of this issue. Recently, Southern Baptist leader Richard Land said on a radio program, "I am not sure that God has anything to say about NAFTA [the North American Free Trade Agreement] or CAFTA [the Central American Free Trade

Agreement], but I am positive He has something to say about the sanctity of life."[1] In short, abortion is wrong, but we cannot necessarily claim a particular Christian perspective on international trade. Nonetheless, there is a great overall guide that Christ gave the world on these and similar matters: do unto others as you would have them do unto you (Matthew 7:12, paraphrase). Jesus will hold us all accountable. Will He not punish those who exploit Chinese factory workers who are forced to toil in subhuman conditions, who are whipped and scourged to meet unreasonable quotas so that we in the West can pay less for their goods? This is especially true for those who are knowingly a part of such a system. Meanwhile, some of the economic proposals to rectify so-called trade imbalances could plunge our economy into a tailspin by cutting us off from the world economy.

How would Jesus have us vote when it comes to health care? This issue is so critical, we will address it in the next chapter.

But to answer these questions more thoroughly, we need to look at some unspoken assumptions that violate the Word of God. These assumptions lie at the root of some of the divisive economic issues being debated today.

Private Property and Work

The Bible is not a textbook on economics. It is not a textbook on politics or science, either. But Scripture has a great deal to say about those subjects. From those teachings, we may erect certain systems and derive an understanding about those subjects. Certainly the Bible has much to say about private property. We have an interest in our own property, Scripture says, and that interest is guarded by the flaming sword of divine vengeance and guaranteed in the Ten Commandments: "You shall not steal" (Exodus 20:15).

God knows that for us to fulfill our probation in this world, it will be necessary for us to make use of the things of this world. If we are going to demonstrate our faithfulness in little things, if we are going to demonstrate our honesty, if we are going to demonstrate our charity, we will need to exercise private ownership. Therefore, God has guaranteed it.

Private ownership rules out certain systems, such as communism or various aspects of socialism that would deprive us of our property rights. The Bible has a good deal to say about other things that impinge upon economic matters as well, such as greed and covetousness and envy and jealousy.

Scripture also has something to say about work. Many people suppose that work is a curse to be avoided, an activity to be involved in only when necessary. But in fact, God ordained work before the fall. Adam was commanded to tend the garden before he fell into sin; therefore, work is not part of the curse (see Genesis 2:15). Even after sin, it is still true that work occupies an important position in our life, though it is greatly aggravated by the results of the fall and the curse (see Genesis 3:17–19). Without work, it is impossible for anyone to fulfill God's purpose for his or her life.

The apostle Paul minces no words about loafers: "For even when we were with you, we commanded you this: If anyone will not work, neither shall he eat" (2 Thessalonians 3:10). The apostle knew that we were inclined toward evil, and so we will avoid all opportunities to work if we can. This does not refer to a person who is unable to work. Scripture has a great deal to say about caring for the lame, the blind, the sick, the infirmed, the aged, and the young, but if anyone *refuses* to work, then neither let him eat.

Most people feel a twinge of guilt when they hear those words, as if they were words without compassion. But this is the most compassionate statement on the subject of economics that has ever been uttered.

Were that dictum not followed to a large degree, famine and starvation would plague the world. So let it be proclaimed to a deaf culture committed to a form of socialism that scholar Rousas Rushdoony calls "the politics of guilt and pity":[2] if one will not work, neither let him eat.

LARGESSE FROM THE TREASURY

In the early 1800s, someone astutely predicted, "America will last until the populace discovers that it can vote for itself largesse out of the public treasury."[3] According to this saying, America will exist only until people realize they can vote gifts or handouts from the public treasury to themselves.

Much of the public has discovered this, and politicians are bending over backward to let the rest of the people know. Often politicians boast about how much money they have steered from the treasury to their constituencies for their pet projects. What few people point out is that this is the people's money, not the politicians' money.

You've seen the commercials saying, "This little booklet will tell you everything you can get out of the federal government." My friend, we are on the way down now because of that, because of the socialism that exists in our mixed economy.

I like the definition of socialism attributed to Winston Churchill: "Capitalism is the unequal distribution of wealth. Socialism is the equal distribution of poverty." We have relinquished the free-enterprise economy the Founders of this nation gave us. We have followed the socialists, albeit a number of paces behind them, down this disastrous road. We are now suffering the consequences. But we have not even begun to see the consequences that are coming if the present trend continues. More important is what the federal government is taking from you and me. The government does not have any money that it does not take from us, and that's a subject many people seem not to understand.

The late conservative journalist Rus Walton commented: "Government is not a producer; it is a taker, a taxer, and a spender. Every dollar spent by the public sector is a dollar the government must take from the private sector, from the workers and earners and investors. The dollar taken by government cannot be spent or invested by that productive private sector."[4]

This is where our problems begin. If we continue the way we are going, we will see even semisocialized nations self-destruct just as the former Soviet Union did. It just may take them a little bit longer.

Though we have seen the Soviet Union come to a disastrous end, socialism is still alive and well in America. We use other names for it like the Welfare State and "a benevolent government," but it's the same thing. The names sound so compassionate, even Christian. We are trying to help people. It is always good intentions that bureaucrats play to that lead us into such disasters. But what we need to understand is that the federal government is inefficient and creates far more problems than it solves. One of America's leading economists, Professor Thomas Sowell of Stanford University, observed: "The amount of money necessary to lift every man, woman, and child in America above the poverty line is *one-third* of what, in fact, is being spent on poverty programs. Clearly, much of the transfer ends up in the pockets of highly paid administrators, consultants and staff."[5] That is why two "bedroom counties" of Washington, D.C. (one in Virginia and one in Maryland) have the highest per capita income in America today.

According to one estimate, the federal government spends twice as much money to create a job as does the private sector. Sometimes it spends far more. For example, the government gave Stanford University $15 million to use to create jobs. With that $15 million, the university created a total of thirty-nine jobs. That averages out to $384,615 per job. The private sector, meanwhile, produces jobs at a cost of $20,000 per job.[6] Thus, the more money we pour into such government jobs projects, that much less money is available to the private sector, and the fewer jobs are created. The more taxes the government takes from the private sector, the fewer jobs are created.

The government is extraordinarily wasteful. Examples of that are so numerous they hardly bear mentioning, but consider that we are spending hundreds of thousands, even millions of dollars, to learn such things as

★ why people cheat and lie on tennis courts;
★ the mating habits of Japanese quail;
★ whether sheepdogs really protect sheep;
★ and all sorts of other "important" things our government wants to know.

In response to all this waste, people say, "Well, yes, but that's what the Bible says we ought to be doing: helping others." Absolutely. But we are not helping them in the way that we should. Instead, we are hurting people: putting them out of work, destroying their families, destroying their children. The Soviet Union found this out to its great regret. And today we are moving happily down that same road.

When you listen to politicians' campaign rhetoric, it becomes clear they are offering the American people specific promises. "Vote for me, and I'll make sure the government gives you XYZ." Of course, XYZ is not free. Money does not grow on trees. So essentially the politicians are promising some sort of redistribution of wealth. Is it not fair to say that they are attempting to buy votes? When politicians say that we need to tax only the very rich, that the rich are not paying their fair share, that tax cuts help only the rich, many Americans buy it. They cannot see the unbiblical assumptions being promoted.

It behooves the discerning Christian voter to think in these terms. Do not take political promises at face value. Evaluate them. Remember, when a politician promises you a benefit, by definition it is at someone else's expense.

CALVIN AND CAPITALISM

My view of economics differs in some of its key premises from what others claim should be the Christian view. I believe in capitalism, but not the dog-eat-dog variety. I certainly do not believe in socialism, which is anything but Christian. The rise of capitalism and free enterprise derives historically, as do many positive aspects of our culture, from the influence of the gospel.

As many historians will tell you, John Calvin can be cited as the founder of capitalism. So tremendous was his influence in the economic realm that he was accused by his detractors (such as Max Weber in his famous work, *The Protestant Ethic and the Spirit of Capitalism*) of all the inequities and distortions of capitalism. The nineteenth-century German theologian Ernst Troeltsch also blamed all of capitalism's faults on Calvin.

Capitalism began to make its rise, at least in a precapitalistic form, in northern Italy and southern Germany prior to Calvin's time. But Calvin was the first theologian who saw the very heart of the matter and was willing to depart from the traditional Roman Catholic Church position that had been held for many centuries, which was influenced by the teachings of Aristotle through Thomas Aquinas, the great theologian who tried to harmonize Christian teaching with Aristotelian views.

About 400 BC, Aristotle taught that money was sterile and nonproductive. This was the view of the Catholic Church. Calvin saw that this was not true; in fact, money could be exceedingly productive. The Catholic Church had defined usury (lending money at an exorbitant rate of interest, which is forbidden by the Bible) as the practice of requiring any interest at all on loaned money (this is still the predominant view of lending money in the Muslim world). Calvin saw that this was neither right nor biblical, and he redefined usury in the sense in which we know it today: that is, the charging of *excessive* interest. Calvin believed that no interest should be charged to the poor, but this was consistent with his view of biblical teaching.

In so doing, Calvin freed money from the bondage in which it had been held for centuries, and he unleashed the power of capitalism. Meanwhile, he saw that money should be used to serve others. He also rebuked the Robin Hood philosophy (robbing the rich to pay the poor). Quoting Calvin, Wheaton College professor Leland Ryken wrote:

> Calvin had already established the same critique of socialism: "The poor…have no right to pillage the wealthy.… God has distributed this world's goods as he has seen fit, and even the richest of all people…shall not be robbed of their possessions by those in direct need."[7]

Some might say, "Calvin must have been a wealthy man who was trying to protect his goods." Hardly. His total estate at his death was valued at about a thousand dollars (at today's rate of exchange).[8] For the well-being of humanity, Calvin knew that the right of private property must be sustained.

Calvin also realized that the Old Testament provided safeguards for those who were unable to work or who were incapable of providing for themselves. It said that the corners of the fields were not to be harvested, and if a person dropped grains of corn as he was harvesting the fields, he was not to go back and pick them up but rather leave these for the needy and the poor. Calvin put these ideas into practice in Geneva and provided help for people in need.

It is important today that we listen, once more, to Calvin's voice regarding the principles in God's Word concerning economics, lest we find ourselves among other fallen nations that have not.

Calvin was not naive enough to assume what Adam Smith assumed in *The Wealth of Nations*—that a laissez faire, or "hands off," form of government capitalism would produce the greatest good for the greatest number of people. Calvin had too clear a view of the sinfulness of human nature and knew there must be restraints. No doubt, in our land today, we have gone far beyond these restraints in the idea of the welfare state.

What then is this economic system that Calvin has given us, based on the Scriptures? What has it produced? What can it do? I read a statement recently that I think is very provocative: "If we had ten millionaires in this country for every one that we now have, the standard of living would be…" I wonder how each of us would finish that sentence. If we had ten millionaires in this country for every one we now have, the general standard of living for the rest of the people would be—what? If you listen to the socialistic voices that are all around us, you would be convinced that the answer to that would be "greatly impoverished." But I believe that the truth, as it is taught in the Scriptures and in the teachings of Calvin, is that the standard of living would be much increased. Why? Because money is not static; it is dynamic and productive. Accumulated capital equals tools, machinery, implements, transportation, and greater resources that would otherwise be unavailable.

DECAPITALIZATION

Probably the greatest woe that could befall any nation materially would be decapitalization, that is, the total equalization of wealth. Think about what that would do. It would plunge the world back into the Dark Ages and result in massive starvation.

Imagine a village built at the edge of a cliff. Three or four hundred feet down from this cliff was a river. Every day each family had to spend about two hours going down to the river with buckets in order to draw water. One man had an idea, though. He noticed that there was another river about five miles behind the cliff. If he could get a pipe from that river to the village, he could bring water to the people and save them the chore of daily having to fetch water. So every evening for years and years, after he had worked all day long on his farm, he would cut pieces of bamboo and fit them together. Finally he had five miles of bamboo pipe that he put into the river above the village. While everybody watched, water flowed into a reservoir that he had prepared in the center of the village.

He sold the water to the people for a sum equivalent to fifteen minutes of their time, and they rejoiced in this. No more backbreaking labor every day to get the water, no more losing two hours each day to fetch water. Everybody had enough water, and the village flourished because the time saved ultimately allowed them to work more and make more money.

Then someone said, "Why should the water man have more than the rest of us? He does not do anything. What we ought to do is put a tax on his pipeline. And then we can have part of his wealth, and we will be better off." So they put a tax on the pipeline, and the next year they increased the tax.

Soon the man, who had been repairing the pipeline whenever it broke, found that it was no longer profitable to own the pipeline. So the next time it broke down, he did not fix it. Soon the reservoir emptied, and the village was back to square one. The crops diminished, productivity dropped off, and the people went back to spending two hours a day fetching water.

There is a biblical principle behind this story. Jesus said, "He who is greatest among you shall be your servant" (Matthew 23:11). Henry Ford made millions of dollars, and yet he enriched the lives of everyone.

ACTS 5

Secular humanists continually cite the need for America to abandon the evil capitalist system in order to become more equitable and charitable. Those who claim that the Bible teaches that capitalism is evil invariably point to Acts 4–5 and the stories of Barnabas and Ananias.

Barnabas sold a piece of land and gave the money from the sale to the apostles. Ananias and his wife sold some land and decided not to give all the proceeds to the apostles. They brought only a portion of the money to the apostles and lied about the price. Is private property repudiated, or is it taught? Notice what Peter said to Ananias: "While [the property] remained, was it not your own?" (Acts 5:4). It is difficult for me to imagine any clearer statement about ownership than that. Clearly we can see that the Bible teaches the right of private property.

Second, note that this action was voluntary. Ananias and his wife did not *have* to sell their property. There was no commandment to sell it. There was no commandment to donate the funds to the church, but they decided to do it. There was great grace upon them, and being so overwhelmed by the grace of God working mightily in their hearts, they did this out of the abundance of their concern.

Third, consider the disposition of the money. They sold the property, and they brought the money, and they "laid it at the apostles' feet" (5:2). I can think of nothing more perfectly designed to give Karl Marx apoplexy than the idea that people should sell all their property and give the money to the church. If there is anything antithetical to the spirit of modern socialism, it would be precisely that. Yet people have the incredible temerity to say that this passage in Acts endorses modern state socialism. Nothing could be further from the truth.

Lastly, we might point out that this spontaneous giving that took place in Jerusalem—the giving and holding of things in common—was never repeated anywhere else. Nor was it ever commanded by God. Indeed, it seems that it was economically unsuccessful. The book of Acts and Paul's epistles show that Paul repeatedly sought offerings throughout the Roman Empire to bring to the poor saints in Jerusalem. Some have speculated that by this socialistic endeavor they impoverished themselves for the next half century.

THE WELFARE STATE

Yes, we are to help people. Churches and charities and private organizations are to help people. When we do it, it does not have a devastating effect. What we should do is try to teach people so they do not have to become the continual, generational recipients of welfare, a system that destroys incentives and the meaning of life for people. This is happening in our country today, not to mention the fact that escalating welfare is causing a deficit that will likely destroy America.

Government welfare programs lessen the ability of the nation to survive. Today we are confronted with an implacable foe in the jihadists, who want to kill us in the name of Allah, and we struggle to find the money to provide an adequate defense against them. Why? Because we are giving away more than a trillion dollars a year in transfer payments of one sort or another (welfare checks, food stamps, school lunch programs, and so on). We do not have the funds to underwrite everyone's needs, and as a result of trying, we may bring about the annihilation of American society.

The Bible teaches freedom and responsibility and work, and yet we are jettisoning all of them in the name of "justice" and "charity." The Bible does not equate justice with charity, which inhibits productivity and puts a damper on the gross national product, throwing people out of work and creating all sorts of economic chaos. It is vitally important for people to understand the difference here. Justice is fairness and impartiality. Justice is blind. It must treat all people equally, without consideration of race, class, or gender. On the other hand, charity is not blind. It is discriminating and voluntary. If you remove the voluntary aspect of charity, it is no longer charity.

Confusing justice and charity has produced social justice, which is the basis for the welfare state. You cannot have charity or justice when you forcibly take money from one person and give it to another. Instead, the rights of each must be protected. Behind this notion of social justice lurks the idea that there must be a more equitable distribution of wealth. When politicians talk about the wealthy paying their "fair share," that notion presupposes the idea of a static, unchanging economic pie chart. This view stipulates that if you have eight people, and one person ends up with a very large piece, justice means we must take part of it to give to the others. That concept has become so prevalent it's hardly questioned anymore. However, in the free enterprise system that has made this country so prosperous, we see that this pie is actually growing every day. If one person ends up with a bigger piece, another person does not have less; he will actually find he has received a bigger piece as well. In contributing to the enlargement of one piece, every other piece also grows.

Consider Henry Ford. If you hold to the idea of a static economic pie, you would think he obtained hundreds of millions of dollars by plundering the nation and impoverishing everyone else by his gain. But, in fact, because of Ford, we are all richer today, able to drive to work, to visit family, and to obtain a greater distribution of goods than is otherwise imaginable. Every one of us enjoys a larger slice of pie today because of Ford.

I find it fascinating to hear the latest starlet who wears a five-thousand-dollar designer dress bad-mouthing the capitalist system. She is shuttled off in her limousine to her multimillion-dollar mansion and has little concept of those she's influencing who know so little about the true economic system that has led to her luxurious life of freedom.

Attempts to correct abuses in the capitalist system have always been necessary. Yet if we are to truly help those in the lower class, we need to realize that the poor are the ones hurt by the politics of guilt and pity. Welfare has chased fathers out of many poor households and condemned single moms to a life of poverty. The poor in America would be much better off without state welfare, since the family is the key to upward mobility. We have spent five trillion dollars on the war on poverty—and we have lost. The welfare state inevitably produces more of that which it sets out to cure. Fifty years ago there were practically no transfer payments or other forms of social spending in this country.

When I preached about this in the early 1980s, there were $283 billion in transfer payments of one sort or another. More recently, adding up the U.S. Treasury's outlays for fiscal year 2000, that number now exceeds $900 billion. And this applies only to *federal* spending; it has nothing to do with state or local wealth-transfer programs.

Let me show how I came to this number:

food assistance programs	$32,687,000,000[9]
public health service	$28,281,000,000
health-care financing	$413,124,000,000
Housing and Urban Development	$30,830,000,000
unemployment trust	$24,149,000,000
Social Security Administration	$441,810,000,000[10]
Total	$970,881,000,000

Nearly one trillion dollars *per year* of taxpayers' money was spent on these different transfer programs, and this list is by no means exhaustive of federal spending for such purposes. So do we have fewer poor people today than when we began all these programs? The answer is no. These programs have hurt the very people they were designed to help. And they have hamstrung the economy for all of us.[11]

Anything the government subsidizes, it increases. If chickens are selling for $1.00 a pound, and the government subsidizes the chicken industry for a $1.50 a pound, what will inevitably happen? In five years you will be up to your armpits in chickens. The same is true with the welfare system. We are going to have more and more people who want in on it.

The truth of this can be seen in the preliminary results of the much-needed welfare reform. These initial reforms have helped many from getting caught in the vicious cycle of poverty. Cheryl Wetzstein writes for the *Washington Times:* "A new study in two states finds that welfare reform is discouraging single mothers from having more children and encouraging them to think 'more seriously about getting married.'"[12] Welfare reform is certainly a step in the right direction.

The welfare state inevitably produces conflict when people begin fighting over receiving a "fair" piece of the pie. Second, the ultimate beneficiaries in public expenditure for welfare are not the recipients but the bureaucrats who administer it. Third, public charity leads to indolence, while private charity encourages a work ethic, because private charity discriminates. Such charity is not likely to benefit a twenty-two-year-old who is living with his parents, loses his job, and then does not look for work. Fourth, public charity and the welfare state destroy private charity. Last year nearly one trillion dollars was expropriated from citizens—money that became unavailable for private charity. What could have been done with that money instead? Fifth, and finally, government dependence leads people to stop depending on God, the Provider. The state becomes the provider for a disbelieving populace.

We are clearly a part of the problem. That is, we the people, including many professing Christians. A new study reported in the *Christian Science Monitor* found that about 53 percent of Americans are on the dole in one way or the other: "Slightly over half of all Americans—52.6 percent—now receive significant income from government programs, according to an analysis by Gary Shilling, an economist in Springfield, N.J. That's up from 49.4 percent in 2000 and far above the 28.3 percent of Americans in 1950."[13] Thus, a majority of Americans have now discovered the ability to extract largesse from the public treasury.

As noted above, in 1996 a Republican Congress, in tandem with a Democrat president, brought us welfare reform. The purpose of this was to alter welfare from being a lifestyle to being a short-term safety net. The reforms limited the time people could be on welfare to two years, with many incentives and much encouragement to develop job skills. This essentially was a very successful measure. It has helped, as opposed to hurt, the poor.

Accumulated capital or profit is transformed into tools and implements, which is what changes the technological twenty-first century from the poverty of the Middle Ages or the conditions that exist in a decapitalized country, such as India. To decapitalize a nation reduces it to a state of third-world living, where most people eke out a living to survive. In the parable of the talents, Jesus said that God has distributed wealth as He has seen fit in His sovereign will, and we are responsible for how we use what we've been given. It is incredible to me that we who live in the greatest economic civilization the world has ever known, vastly better off than most nations in the world, are willing to trade our economic well-being for a system that has reduced the quality of life in every nation in which it's been tried.

Again, God has said that we are to work. This is a God-given privilege. We are to be responsible for how we work and what we accomplish, and we are to offer it all up to the glory of God. And if we are faithful and work hard and save our money, we will produce more tools for economic growth by putting our money in a bank, because that money goes out into industry and produces tools that enable people to make a living. It is because some people have been frugal and saved that the level of all our lives has been uplifted. This is what Jesus said, that we are to put it out and make a profit and use it for the glory of God.

CONCLUSION

How would Jesus want us vote when it comes to economics? I believe He would want us to honor private property. I believe He would want us to do what we can to create an atmosphere that encourages work. I believe He would want His church (in a voluntary way) to help the poor and the downtrodden. I believe He would also want us to be discerning about the political promises we are bombarded with.

I believe that Jesus would encourage private, church-based, community-based giving and financial assistance. I believe He would not favor governmental welfare programs. Such programs have a vested interest in the continuation of poverty, because if the problem of poverty is solved, then the money is no longer needed and the program might end. This is what caused Ronald Reagan to joke, "The nearest thing to eternal life we will ever see on this earth is a government program." If the government's welfare program succeeded, the bureaucrats would be out of a job.

It is one thing to say that Jesus wants us to do more than our fair share for the poor. It is another thing to say that He wants us to use the fist of government to distribute those benefits. Let the government get out of the charity business, and let the family, churches, and communities be free to take care of the less fortunate. I believe we should vote in accordance with true justice and not the mistaken notion of social justice.

I think we can make a substantial difference at the ballot box by studying the issues. We can avoid the "solutions" that leverage our children's and grandchildren's futures by ringing up a large tab in social-transfer payments, like perpetual welfare and meaningless government programs that spend more and more of the taxpayers' money.

Yet again, what we need to realize is that the problem with economics lies within us, in our own hearts—our greed, our desires for getting something for nothing—when we clamor for more and more from the "free" government trough. It is the basis of many of America's financial problems today. However, if our eyes are open to the colossal wastefulness, the mounting federal debt, and the inefficiency and ineffectiveness of government programs, we would know that when our politicians tell us they are going to tax the rich to feed the poor, we should not vote for those candidates. It is only in cutting taxes and government spending that our economic situation improves.

Health-Care Issues

But a certain Samaritan…had compassion.
So he went to him and bandaged his wounds.

—LUKE 10:33–34

How would Jesus have us vote when it comes to health care? I believe strongly that He would want His followers to be very concerned about health care. However, again, as in the previous chapter on economics, the question is, How much, if any, would He want us to enlist the government to get involved in health care? Superficially, some may naively assume that since Jesus wants us to be Good Samaritans to our neighbors, He would want the government to provide free health care.

HEALTH-CARE ISSUES IN CONTEMPORARY AMERICA

Health care in America is in need of reform, most Americans would agree. The questions are, How much reform is needed, and what's the best prescription for change?

Former President Bill Clinton attempted a comprehensive overhaul of the U.S. health-care system. On the campaign trail, he remarked: "We've got to take a dramatically different approach to the health care crisis."[1] But critics wondered if the health-care reform put forth by the Clinton administration was exactly what the doctor ordered.

As of this writing, the Clinton administration's ambitious plan was the most wide-ranging attempt to overhaul the health-care system, so we want to examine that attempt and its underlying assumptions. Some politicians would still like to see such changes made. *NewsMax* reports, "[Hillary Clinton] still wants the same program. She just wants it in stages."[2]

Ed Haislmaier of the Heritage Foundation, a conservative think tank in Washington, D.C., pointed out at the time the proposed bill was under consideration: "The Clinton health plan is in my view an incredibly complicated bureaucratic system for the government controlling health care in this country. Bureaucracy does not work very well in a lot of areas, such as education and welfare. And I don't see any indication that it's going to work better in health care. The president's plan on health care is based on the idea that government knows what's best, government will decide what health care people get; they will decide how much the doctors and hospitals are paid, and they'll decide who gets it and how it's delivered."[3]

WHAT ABOUT THE UNINSURED?

A major justification given for health-care reform is the fact that millions of Americans are without health insurance. In 1993/94, when the Clinton health-care plan was under consideration, some thirty-seven million Americans were purportedly without health insurance. Today, the new number being bandied about is forty-seven million.

Burke Balch is a state legislative director for the National Right to Life, an organization on record as opposing the Clinton health-care plan because it would have forced government to get into the abortion business and would have likely forced the government into the euthanasia business as well. Balch observed that the thirty-seven-million figure is misleading:

> There certainly is a problem with people who are uninsured in our country today, but most people misunderstand the magnitude of

that problem. You hear the figure 37 million uninsured. The reality is: virtually all of those people are temporarily uninsured because they're between jobs. Only about 890,000 people are truly un-insured because they're [allegedly] "uninsurable." They have AIDS or they have cancer or something of that nature. Now, that's an important group of people. You know, it's less than a million, they certainly need to be treated and need to be helped, but to suggest that in order to do that, we need to ration care for everybody sim-ply is ridiculous.[4]

PRO-LIFE CONCERNS

Those politicians who want the government to get into the health-care business tend to be "the government is the answer" types who favor abor-tion on demand. Most of those who opposed the Clinton health-care plan in the early 1990s were part of the pro-life movement. That particular health-care plan would have most certainly enshrined abortion rights. At the time, U.S. Congressman Chris Smith of New Jersey said, "Clinton's health plan talks about reproductive health, doesn't even mention the word abortion, but everyone knows, and this has been affirmed on the record by high Clinton appointees, that this means abortion on demand at any time during pregnancy, and you and I and other taxpayers will pay for it."[5]

Burke Balch read the fine print on how the Clinton health-care plan could have affected the right-to-life issue: "The co-payments would be as little as $10 to get an abortion. It would be almost less expensive than using methods of family planning. So we'll see the number of abortions rocket up from the 1.6 million that occur every year."[6]

Abortion would be even harder to stop if the government essentially started to subsidize it.

A DANGEROUS ETHIC

Abortion as a means of birth control does not belong to the sanctity-of-life ethic; it is part of the quality-of-life ethic, which is inherent in the Clinton health-care plan. This dangerous ethic is founded upon the idea that only those with a specified quality of life are worthy to receive health care. Syndicated columnist Cal Thomas commented:

> This means that the government, based on a formula it will come up with, will decide basically who shall live and who shall die. Now they'll begin as they usually do in these sorts of cases with the extreme cases: 98 year old Alzheimer's and cancer sufferers with multiple kidney dysfunctions, and then everybody will agree that maybe we shouldn't spend several millions of dollars to extend that kind of life. But it will be a very short move from that, as we've seen with abortion, and increasingly with infanticide, to the government deciding *your* life is no longer valuable, therefore, we are not going to pay to sustain it.[7]

Again, Congressman Chris Smith warned: "We're setting in motion the rationing of health care in America under the Clinton plan, and it's almost as sure as night follows day and day follows night that we will have an active euthanasia program within a time certain if this were to succeed."[8]

LOOK AT EUROPE

Unfortunately, we are already seeing this trend in some countries with socialized medicine that have also bought into the quality-of-life ethic, such as the Netherlands and England. Retired Dutch physician Richard Fenigsen commented on euthanasia in Holland: "The number of patients who are being killed by doctors without a request is slightly higher than the number of patients being killed upon request."[9]

Mercy killing began in Holland in a voluntary way. You want to be killed? Fine, they will kill you. But as more doctors became professional killers instead of professional healers, the number of patients who were killed against their will or the will of their loved ones (if the patients could not speak for themselves) exceeded the number of those killed voluntarily. This is the frightening reality to which Fenigsen was alluding. When the state chooses who will live and who will die, we all lose. Certainly, we lose all sense of Christian morality at that point.

THE HOSPITAL AND THE CHURCH

We should never forget that health care as an institution is heavily indebted to the church. It was during the Christian era that hospitals as we know them were born. The longest continuously running hospital in the world is the Hotel Dieu, which is close to Notre Dame. They share the same public square. Hotel Dieu means "Hotel God." Many hospitals were started by Christians to help the sick in Jesus's name. Since our Lord healed the sick, His followers sought to heal the sick as well. (Of course, He did magnificent miracles. We can only attempt to do magnificent works of mercy.)

Paul Maier, professor of ancient history at Western Michigan University, is a best-selling author and a first-rate Christian apologist. He observed: "Hospitals were virtually invented by the Christian church. Before this, the best they could do was to drag sick people into the temple of Asclepius in Greece and then get them all together, and the contagion would spread, of course. Christianity came along and virtually invented the hospital system, whereby the sick would be taken care of and ministered to on the basis of the love of Jesus Christ, which should be shared."[10]

Many of today's hospitals were begun and are run by churches or denominations or religious orders. They have Christian names like Christ Hospital, Baptist Hospital, Holy Cross, Good Samaritan, St. Mary's, and so on.

AVOIDANCE OF HOSPITALS?

Tragically, in places like the Netherlands, where the health establishment has bought into the quality-of-life ethic, some patients, particularly the elderly, avoid going to hospitals. If this sounds far-fetched, remember that forced euthanasia has exceeded the number of voluntary mercy killings in that country. Indeed, many elderly patients in the Netherlands are afraid even to go to a doctor. Several years ago we broadcast a brief interview with a Netherlander who nursed his wife at home for fear that, if he took her to a hospital, they would kill her. "It would be good to put a sign in front of hospital: 'Whoever enters this house, he better let go all his hope.' My wife is sometimes saying to us, I feel I'm being a burden to you all. But I say to her that no, I don't feel at all like that."[11]

Meanwhile, in England, socialized medicine has come to mean health-care rationing and long waiting lists. Burke Balch observed: "In Great Britain right now, anyone who is over 65 has almost no chance of getting kidney dialysis. Here in the United States right now, it's virtually routine."[12] Similarly, Ed Haislmaier observed: "Right now in Britain, there are over 1 million people waiting for medical care, waiting for operations that they need for conditions which are not immediately life-threatening. If you're hit by a bus, you're taken care of. But people who need hip replacements, cataract surgery, heart surgery, transplants, gall bladder surgery, orthopedic surgery, knees, elbows, surgery on the hand, major oral surgery. These are the people who wind up on waiting lists."[13] These observations were made in the early 1990s. The statistics have only gotten worse.

The contrast between socialized medicine and privately funded health care is great. For example, in Broward County, Florida, where I live, there are more MRI machines in the *county* than in the entire *country* of Canada.[14]

Christopher Ruddy, editor in chief of *NewsMax* magazine, noted: "When you hear how efficiently socialized medicine works in Britain or Canada, always remember that almost all the innovations in medicine and drugs that make those systems work at the most basic level came from the United States, which has resisted socialized medicine for a long time. Bring full socialized medicine to America, and this scientific progress will be stunted. All of us will suffer."[15]

Columnist Mark Steyn provides another example where socialized medicine does not work well. He wrote about the socialized medicine policies of Governor Schwarzenegger:

> His state's emergency rooms have been reduced to Quebec-level waiting times because of the strains of providing free health care to the legions of the undocumented Americans. One-third of the patients in Los Angeles County hospitals are illegal immigrants, and they've overwhelmed the system. Dozens of emergency rooms in the state have closed this decade after degenerating into an unfounded de facto Mexican health-care network. If you're a legal resident of California, your health system is worse than it was a decade ago and will be worse still in a decade's time.[16]

WHEN HEALTH-CARE RATIONING PROVES FATAL

This health-care rationing can even be fatal for those deemed to have a poor quality of life. Burke Balch commented on a tragic case:

> In England, for example, a child was born with cerebral palsy and other disabilities, and the parents wanted that child to live, but the health care authorities said, no, we don't think this child's life is worth living, and that child died. That's the sort of person who will die if the Clinton health care plan is enacted. One of the ironies of the Clinton health care rationing plan is that while it will pay to detect children with disabilities in the womb and pay for their abortions, if a child is born with a disability, the plan will not cover rehabilitative treatment for that child. So the financial incentives will be to kill children with disabilities, not to treat them.[17]

If the government gets into the health-care business, all of these nightmare scenarios have a real possibility of becoming the norm. This may sound far-fetched, but consider: when the government has to make the financial decisions in dealing with scarce, limited resources, then it will have to make life-or-death decisions as well. Handicapped infants, and handicapped adults, for that matter, could easily become victims, set aside for premature death.

MIRACLE BABY

These kinds of life-or-death decisions are all too real to Bev and Randy Larson of Hollywood, Florida. The proposal for the government to take over the nation's health care could easily mean life and death for children like their seventeen-year-old daughter, Samantha. When Bev was pregnant with Samantha, her doctor pressured her to abort. A sonogram revealed that the unborn baby had spina bifida, a condition in which the spinal cord fails to close properly.

Bev said, "The baby had developed hydrocephalous, which was what they had feared, and the doctor had found that the baby had 76 percent water on the brain by taking a ratio of the circumference of the head. It was very apparent that the baby was going to have a hard time developing a brain."

Randy noted that he, too, was being pressured to have his wife abort the baby. "I had people from the medical field saying how this baby's gonna cost so much to society, you know, all the operations, and how that's going to be taken away from people with healthy children, and is it really fair to do that to society?"

Bev added, "The doctor had really confronted me, and though I was nearly five months along, he was recommending an abortion, and I said that I just wouldn't have an abortion."

When health care is rationed, and this is inevitably what will happen if the government takes over the health-care system, all the Samanthas of this world will be aborted, despite the opinions and beliefs of the parents.

The Larsons, who are otherwise shy, stood up in front of their church of some two thousand members and asked the people to pray for their unborn child. Bev said, "And the next week [after all the prayer], when we had the sonogram, the doctor, the technician said, 'If I didn't know this child had spina bifida, I couldn't tell it now.' And Randy and I were, like, are we going to have a full-fledged miracle? And then it happened that the spine was still open, but the bubble had disappeared. And not only that, but the water on the brain had gone down, and the doctor said, 'In all my years of practice, I've never seen water on the brain go down. It only gets worse.'"

When Samantha was born, there was great rejoicing in the delivery room. She has had minor problems, such as needing to wear leg braces, but none of that has changed the fact that she is a wonderful gift from God. To Bev and Randy, who can't imagine their lives without their little girl, the thought of what could happen to future Samanthas under socialized medicine is disturbing and frightening.

Bev commented: "It seems our society is getting more and more like what Hitler was trying to do in sifting out all the unwanteds in society. Babies don't have to be perfect to be a blessing. You're never guaranteed a blueprint of perfection when you're carrying a child. Anything that is written to say we will hold back care from a catastrophic deformity or a child who's going to be knowingly born with a birth defect, what is the value behind that? It's not life. I think God should be the one to decide that, not man."[18]

CONCLUSION

How would Jesus vote when it comes to health care? I certainly believe He would be concerned about the plight of those who are uninsured. I certainly believe He would support those voluntary programs in which Christians share their medical expenses with each other. But I do not believe He would want the government to decide who receives health care, forcing services to be rationed.

Christopher Ruddy wrote, "There are better solutions to the health-care crisis. The private health savings account (HAS) is one. These accounts empower consumers. Another is the use of private charity to help serve the needs of the poor. Regardless of what we choose, one thing is sure: Socialized medicine is not the answer."[19]

Interestingly, the price of health care has skyrocketed during the last few decades. Why? Certainly, runaway lawsuits have contributed to the costs.

Certainly, inflation has played a role. But perhaps the biggest overall increases have come because of government involvement in health care, beginning with Medicare and Medicaid. The federal government has forced all of us to pay exorbitant prices. Who does this hurt the most? The poor. For the government, with all its inefficiency, to take over health care in this country—especially when it imposes an anti-Christian ethic, such as forcing abortions on handicapped unborn children or forcing euthanasia on the weak—strikes me as fundamentally anti-Christian. Therefore, be careful when casting your vote.

The Environment and Climate Change

*Then God said, "Let Us make man in Our image,
according to Our likeness;
let them have dominion over the fish of the sea,
over the birds of the air, and over the cattle,
over all the earth and over every creeping thing
that creeps on the earth."*

—GENESIS 1:26

Scientists have warned us about the precarious state of the globe. The signs are all around. They declare:

> There are ominous signs that the Earth's weather patterns have begun to change dramatically and that these changes may portend a drastic decline in food production—with serious political implications for just about every nation on Earth.... The evidence in support of these predictions has now begun to accumulate so massively that meteorologists are hard-pressed to keep up with it.... Climatologists are pessimistic that political leaders will take any positive action to compensate for the climatic change, or even to allay its effects.... The longer the planners delay, the more difficult will they find it to cope with climatic change once the results become grim reality.[1]

So what are we to do? The evidence is overwhelming—most scientists agree. We can no longer afford to delay our efforts to save the earth. Should we be aggressive about fighting global warming?

This dire prediction about the coming climate change is actually from a 1975 *Newsweek* article—when global *cooling* was supposedly the big environmental threat. It may seem strange now, but scientists in 1975 believed that world temperatures were falling and would continue to fall. Their research seemed to indicate the world had been cooling since the 1940s. Yet later, popular opinion reversed, and predictions resumed about global-warming trends that began in the 1880s.

Those committed to a biblical worldview understand that God made the world, and it does not hang in the balance. The world He made goes through warming and cooling periods that have nothing to do with human activities. It is simply human hubris when we declare that we are the cause of global warming (or cooling).

What we are experiencing at the present time is what two scientists have labeled "unstoppable global warming every 1,500 years."[2] Rising and falling temperatures are cyclical. If there is a villain in this scenario, it is the sun, not the SUV. Even Mars is experiencing global warming at present because of the sun.

In this chapter we want to explore global warming, which has become a hot topic among Christian voters.

SPLITTING THE EVANGELICAL VOTE?

In February 2006 a group of about eighty prominent evangelicals—including Rick Warren, author of *The Purpose-Driven Life,* and Duane Litfin, president of Wheaton College—signed a document called the Evangelical Climate Initiative (ECI). The document focused on curbing what it said were human causes of global warming, in part because of global warming's alleged impact on the world's poor.[3]

But while the document may have given the impression that there was consensus in the evangelical community, the reality is that many (if not most) evangelicals disagree with the conclusions outlined in the ECI. In 1999 some

130 evangelical leaders, including James Dobson, Charles Colson, Richard Land, Don Wildmon, and me, signed the Cornwall Declaration,[4] arguing that science itself is not clear that human activity is to blame for global warming. E. Calvin Beisner, a professor at Knox Theological Seminary and spokesman for the Cornwall Alliance for the Stewardship of Creation (which was formed to promote the principles expressed in the Cornwall Declaration), argued that the poor would suffer more from Kyoto Protocol–type policies to combat global warming than from the actual phenomenon itself.

The environment is a divisive issue, and today we can find concerned and well-meaning Christians on different sides of the debate. But I am disappointed that conservatives have largely abandoned the field to the liberals. There is a strong biblical argument to be made for why development and free markets are the best way to bring about charitable, compassionate Christian results for everyone, including developing countries. There is also an argument to be made about what exactly constitutes a "good environment."

Arguments rage within the scientific community about how to determine whether we are witnessing naturally occurring climate change or a more sinister form of human-caused global warming. Some use the phrase *climate change* to attribute freak occurrences of nature to our use of fossil fuels.

What exactly is normal when it comes to climate change? Are we really seeing a dire situation emerge, or are we simply living through one of nature's regular cycles? It seems to me that if someone complains, "Boy, it's really hot out," the reply is, "That's global warming." If someone says, "Wow, it's cold out today," again it's attributed to global warming. John Rabe of our staff wisely observed that this is a tautology—anything that happens, no matter what it is, is attributed to a single theory. And if a lone theory can explain everything, it explains nothing.

If I were to agree that the assumptions of the ECI are correct, then I would not hesitate to support its conclusions. ECI believes that "most of the climate change problem is human induced." Furthermore, it predicts that "millions of people could die in this century."[5] Again, if I thought the ECI was correct, I would sign it. But I think the science on which the ECI statement is based is not as clear as Al Gore's award-winning film *An Inconvenient Truth* would have us believe.

A HUGE DIVIDE

There is a huge divide in the understanding of mankind and earth. Are humans a divinely appointed steward of the earth, as we see in God's statement at the creation (see Genesis 1:26)? Or are humans a freak of nature who have crawled out of the primordial slime but who have managed to lord it over the lower creatures because they could?

How Christians respond to environmental issues often boils down to one of these two starting points: creation or evolution.

God is the Creator. To rape the environment is an insult to His creation. We must remember the first principle of stewardship...which is what? How would you answer that?

"The earth is the LORD's, and all its fullness, the world and those who dwell therein" (Psalm 24:1). It all belongs to God. He created it, He sustains it, it is His, and wonder of wonders, He allows us to use it. He blesses us with good seasons and rain and all of the things that are needful. We are His stewards on this planet, and He will one day hold us accountable.

To rape the environment is a sin. God calls us to be stewards of creation. But it does not follow that Christians who are concerned about the earth should get on board the latest environmentalist bandwagon.

Many today say that we live in a time where the very continuation of the world is in doubt. We are poisoning the atmosphere. We are poisoning the water. We are poisoning the ground with atomic slag. Indeed, there seems to be no future for the earth. We are destroying the ozone layer, and we are melting the polar icecaps.

Again, if I were convinced that global warming was a product of human activity, I would be raising my voice to fight it. But we don't know this. As a result, the global-warming issue is overblown. However, the global-warming issue has become so politically correct that there is no fair media coverage of the other side of the debate. This reminds me of the time a janitor found a minister's notes the day after the sermon was preached. There was a handwritten note in the margin: "Argument Weak. Pound pulpit here!" It helps no one to be dogmatic about an issue in which credentialed scientists come down on all sides.

Senator James Inhofe, a Republican from Oklahoma, recently distributed a press release in which he quoted from *Grist* magazine's online publication. On September 19, 2006, *Grist* staff writer David Roberts quoted the following excerpt from George Monbiot's new book "about the climate change 'denial industry'" entitled *Heat: How to Stop the Planet from Burning.*

When we've finally gotten serious about global warming, when the impacts are really hitting us and we're in a full worldwide scramble to minimize the damage, we should have war crimes trials for these bast---s—some sort of climate Nuremberg.[6]

Inhofe quoted those who call people like me "global warming deniers." I don't appreciate that language, which is meant to evoke the language used against Holocaust deniers. One recent article on the debate was entitled "Global Warming: The Chilling Effect on Free Speech."[7] The stakes on this issue are too important for us to suppress real and honest debate.

Such political gamesmanship should send chills up your spine. Not all scientists agree with the science du jour of global warming (or that human activity causes global warming), but social elites want to punish those who do not agree with the politically correct view.

Former vice president Al Gore gives the impression in *An Inconvenient Truth* that scientists agree that global warming is caused by human activity and that, if humans did the right thing, we could slow down the trend. The Cornwall Alliance, however, says that is far from the case. Cornwall claims that more than seventeen thousand scientists, two-thirds with advanced degrees, have signed the Oregon Petition, which states: "There is no convincing scientific evidence that human release of carbon dioxide, methane, or other greenhouse gasses is causing or will, in the foreseeable future, cause catastrophic heating of the Earth's atmosphere and disruption of the Earth's climate."[8] Thus, the global warming scare is far from settled science.

DOMINION OVER NATURE

According to the Bible, God has given human beings dominion over the earth. The psalmist says to the God of mankind:

> You have made him to have dominion over the works of
>   Your hands;
> You have put all things under his feet,
> All sheep and oxen—
> Even the beasts of the field,

> The birds of the air,
>
> And the fish of the sea
>
> That pass through the paths of the seas. (Psalm 8:6–8)

What is mankind? We are princes and princesses in a royal realm. Our origin is from the heart and mind of God, and our destiny is in paradise forever.

Environmental extremists have a different view of man. Instead of seeing humans as God-given stewards to the earth, they see man as the cause of all the earth's problems, including global warming. Paul Watson, the founder and president of the Sea Shepherd Conservation Society, wrote an editorial for the society's Web site in May 2007 in which he compares humans to a virus on the planet. In fact, we are the "AIDS of the earth":

> Humans are presently acting upon this body [the earth's ecosystem] in the same manner as an invasive virus with the result that we are eroding the ecological immune system.
>
> A virus kills its host and that is exactly what we are doing with our planet's life support system. We are killing our host the planet Earth.
>
> I was once severely criticized for describing human beings as being the "AIDS of the Earth." I make no apologies for that statement. Our viral like behaviour can be terminal both to the present biosphere and ourselves.[9]

Granted, Watson expressed an extreme position, but he began with a godless perspective. Much of today's environmental movement begins with a godless premise, and we need to keep that in mind.

We are not to abuse the trust of creation given to us by the Creator. Obviously, pollution is an abuse of that trust. In the main, I believe that under the free enterprise system we have been able to correct many of the pollutants in our country.

In a country like Haiti, the poorest nation in the Western Hemisphere, we see an extreme case of what happens when humans rape their environment. The country was once beautiful, but between the French despoiling of the "Pearl of the Antilles" (as Haiti was once known) and a succession of corrupt governments, Haiti today is a far different place.

The problems in Haiti are plain to see: for one, people have cut down too many trees. This has had devastating consequences for the struggling nation, but primarily it has ruined their agriculture. When it rains, it floods. Haiti is an ecological nightmare and a political and economic one as well.

How should we view our environment? Some radical ecologists, environmentalists, and Gaia theorists prefer to worship the earth, that which was created, rather than the Creator. They view the environment as a living entity. But the Christian view of creation is different, perhaps best articulated by Francis of Assisi, who called earth our sister and viewed humans and nature as united creations under God the Father. This view is Creator-oriented rather than earth-oriented.

BABIES OR BIRDS?

What's even more confusing is that some people seem to care more about our planet than they do human life. Christians should esteem both babies and birds, because both are created by God. But not everyone sees things this way.

A press release from the Christian Newswire in 2006 asks: "Why would a pro-abortion foundation want to fund an Evangelical Christian initiative to fight global warming?"[10] The article goes on to provide the answer: "That question is raised in *From Climate Control to Population Control: Troubling Background on the 'Evangelical Climate Initiative,'* a new paper jointly released by the Acton Institute for the Study of Religion and Liberty and the Institute on Religion and Democracy.... 'Our fear is that evangelical leaders, who in good faith associated themselves with the ECI, are being exploited by organizations that not only deny their biblically-based value system, but hold such beliefs in contempt,' said Jay Richards, Ph.D., a research fellow at Acton."[11]

Who actually paid for ECI to get off the ground? Pro-abortion forces, according to the Acton Institute and the Institute on Religion and Democracy. The article continues:

> One of the largest funders of the ECI effort was the William and Flora Hewlett Foundation. The Hewlett Foundation, which contributed $475,000 to the ECI, is a major contributor to the causes of abortion and population control. The Hewlett Foundation funds both environmental and population control groups not by coincidence, but because it thinks that an increase in human population must degrade the environment.
>
> The foundation's population project is focused on "helping women and families choose the number and spacing of children, protecting against sexually transmitted infections, and eliminating unsafe abortion." Such language is a thinly veiled defense of abortion-on-demand, which the Hewlett Foundation supports generously.
>
> James Tonkowich, president of the Institute on Religion and Democracy, pointed out that there is a long history of environmentalist thinking that sees humans primarily as consumers and polluters.

"That thinking leads many to insist that abortion rights are integral to any environmental agenda," he said. "By contrast, we affirm that Earth was shaped by a benevolent Creator to be the habitat that sustains and enriches all human life, even as humans subdue and enrich the Earth through our creativity and industry."[12]

If Christians are to make our way through the confusing and conflicting arguments surrounding the issue of global warming, we will need to keep our focus on both the Creator and the creation. Focusing on one without the other leads to positions that lack balance and perspective.

WHAT ABOUT THE POOR?

As we pointed out earlier, some evangelicals believe that global warming will have a profound impact on the world's poorest people. But E. Calvin Beisner of the Cornwall Alliance believes that measures designed to combat global warming would actually hurt the world's poor far more. Sheryl Henderson Blunt elaborated on this point in a *Christianity Today* article:

> A new coalition argues Christians need not heed warnings that millions will die from human-induced global warming and says we should seek more practical ways to help the world's poor.
>
> Human emissions of carbon dioxide are not the main cause of global warming, the Interfaith Stewardship Alliance (ISA) [the group now known as the Cornwall Alliance for the Stewardship of Creation] said in a document released in July [2006]. The ISA, a loosely affiliated group of more than 130 theologians, scientists, policy analysts, and others, said the consequences of global warming for the poor have been exaggerated....

The ISA is responding to the Evangelical Climate Initiative's February statement "Climate Change: An Evangelical Call to Action," signed by 97[13] evangelical leaders. The statement claimed that "[m]illions of people could die in this century because of climate change, most of them our poorest global neighbors."[14]

Again, the Cornwall Alliance (the former ISA) disputes the scientific assumptions of that evangelical statement, as the *Christianity Today* article points out:

"It's not so much that we have evidence that there won't be global warming; it's that the theories that support catastrophic global warming are so uncertain," said climatologist Roy Spencer, an atmospheric scientist who consults for NASA and co-authored the ISA report. "The public is being misled by those who claim we can greatly reduce global warming by conserving energy, reducing emissions, and buying hybrid cars."[15]

The article goes on to say that if the Kyoto Protocol provisions (measures adopted by many nations to combat global warming) are implemented, they might actually hurt the poor rather than help them. Blunt added:

Beisner said evangelicals should focus on helping the poor create wealth and providing them with clean drinking water and medical care. Efforts to fight global warming could ultimately harm the poor more than help them, according to [Wayne] Grudem.

"If we are forced to reduce production of carbon dioxide, it means that everything that is manufactured or transported has to use more expensive forms of energy," he said. "That drives up the prices of goods around the world and hurts everybody—the poor most of all."[16]

This point needs to be proclaimed loudly and clearly. Jesus said that we should be as "wise as serpents and harmless as doves" (Matthew 10:16). It is unwise to fall prey to alarmist messages, which is often tempting for evangelicals to do because so many have an apocalyptic mentality. The Cornwall Alliance elaborates further in its literature about how efforts to abide by the Kyoto Protocols hurt the poor and do not help them:

> Efforts to cut greenhouse gases hurt the poor. By making energy less affordable and accessible, mandatory emissions reductions would drive up the costs of consumer products, stifle economic growth, cost jobs, and impose especially harmful effects on the Earth's poorest people. The Kyoto climate treaty, for example, could cost the world community $1 trillion a year—five times the estimated price of providing sanitation and clean drinking water to poor developing countries.[17]

Yes, we should try to help the poor. But let us do so in a way that uses our heads and not our emotions, lest we fall for the latest politically correct cause. And let us follow the example of Mother Teresa, who in the name of Jesus, rolled up her sleeves and gave her life to directly help those in need.

CONCLUSION

How would Jesus vote on the environment? He would want us to take care of the earth and be responsible. He would ask us to be discerning about what is true and what is unknown in the current debate. He certainly would be concerned about the impact of proposed environmental measures on the poor. But I believe allocating monetary resources to help build sewage treatment plants, enhance sanitation, and provide clean water for poor people would have a greater immediate impact on their plight than would the battle over global warming.

11

Immigration and Racial Prejudice

*I was a stranger
and you took Me in.*

—Matthew 25:35

I mmigration is undoubtedly a divisive issue. How would Jesus have us consider this matter? One person asked the question this way: Who would Jesus deport? Or at least that's what the individual's T-shirt said after an incident in Chicago in which an illegal immigrant from Latin America sought sanctuary in a church.

One difficult aspect of this issue is the fact that there are as many as twelve million illegal immigrants in America, defying the laws of our nation. Should we penalize would-be immigrants who play by the rules (not breaking the law) by, in the name of compassion, allowing others to simply disobey the laws? Meanwhile, what do we do with those who are already here illegally?

Relatively few illegal immigrants are criminals, but the impact of their criminal activity is significant, says WorldNetDaily's Joseph Farah:

> While the military "quagmire" in Iraq was said to tip the scales of power in the U.S. midterm elections, most Americans have no idea more of their fellow citizens—men, women and children— were murdered this year by illegal aliens than the combined death toll of U.S. troops in Iraq and Afghanistan since those military campaigns began.

Though no federal statistics are kept on murders or any other crimes committed by illegal aliens, a number of groups have produced estimates based on data collected from prisons, news reports and independent research.[1]

Immigration is a thorny issue, but as with all things, the Bible has something to say.

WHAT DOES THE BIBLE SAY?

While the words *immigrant* and *immigration* do not appear in the Bible, this does not mean the issue is not to be found in the Scriptures. Dr. Gary Cass is the former director of the Center for Reclaiming America for Christ. He taught me and many others much about the immigration issue:

> Grace is especially required on this highly emotional subject. It is always wise to begin by carefully examining our motives and not prejudging those of others. Healthy scriptural debate is often stifled by the accusations of crypto-racism or being hyperpatriotic, an ultranationalist or a bleeding heart, a naive liberal or a simpleton do-gooder. Most Christians just play it safe and say nothing, for fear of criticism.
>
> However, the Bible is not silent on this matter. Christ himself has spoken to this issue! So let us seek the grace to humbly submit to his Word. Every good faith question and honest biblical argument needs to be politely considered. This is a great exercise. It will cause Christians to become more self-conscious of their own preconceived ideas or presuppositions. The next step is to submit

those presuppositions to rigorous biblical analysis. Any nonbiblical thoughts or prejudices ought to be rejected, taken captive, and made obedient to Christ.

Some of the seminal questions that deserve biblical answers include, Does God grant the state the authority to enforce borders? If so, who then can they lawfully exclude from their boundaries and for what reasons? In an age of terrorism, what is the duty of the State in how it protects its citizens? The church of the Brethren teaches: God made people—people made borders. Is that true, and if so, what does it imply for our Christian duty?[2]

I would argue that a country does have the right to protect itself from those who would harm it. But that does not mean we support racism. Let me explain.

NO RACISM IN THE KINGDOM OF GOD

Although Christians have surely not lived up to our ideal, there is to be no racism in the kingdom of God. The Bible declares, "And He has made from one blood every nation of men to dwell on all the face of the earth, and has determined their preappointed times and the boundaries of their dwellings" (Acts 17:26). This means that the white man is related to the black man and to every human race in between.

Gary Cass adds this observation on Jesus and immigration: "As we consider the ideas of immigration, we ought to always do so in a Christ-centered way. There is a sense in which we can speak of Christ Jesus, in His becoming a man by His incarnation, as a kind of heavenly stranger (Greek: *xenos* from which we get *xenophobia*—the fear of strangers).

Though He created all things, including this world, yet we can accurately say that Jesus came to save and redeem His creatures as a kind of temporary, resident alien and foreigner."

He points out that there are three major New Testament terms associated with modern notions of immigrants: *foreigners, pilgrims,* and *strangers.* Here is what they mean and the Greek words from which they derive:

The concept of a foreigner comes from the Greek word *par-oikos.* It literally means to have a home (*oikos*) near or beside (*para*); in other words, to be a "by-dweller." This corresponds to our idea of a resident alien. Abraham's descendants were resident aliens in Egypt. God was faithful to preserve them, deliver them, and bring them to the Promised Land in Canaan. ("But God spoke in this way: that his descendants would *dwell in a foreign land,* and that they would bring them into bondage and oppress them four hundred years" [Acts 7:6].)

This same word is used of Moses. After Moses delivered a fellow Jew from the oppression of an Egyptian, Pharaoh sought to kill Moses. He then fled from Egypt and was a resident alien in Midian. ("Then, at this saying, Moses fled and became a *dweller* in the land of Midian, where he had two sons" [Acts 7:29].)

The apostle Peter appeals to believers to live a holy, spiritual life by reminding them that they are only sojourners (Greek: *para-oikos,* a temporary resident). He combines it with another familiar term, *pilgrim* (*parepidemos,* an alien alongside, that is, a resident foreigner). We are to live as those who understand that we are only passing through this world on our way to our glorious eternal home in heaven.

In fact, 1 Peter 2:11 is the source from which the Pilgrims who founded Plymouth Plantation derived their name: "Beloved, I beseech you as strangers and pilgrims, abstain from fleshly lusts, which war against the soul"

(KJV). And there are other examples like this, such as Ephesians 2:11–13, 19 and Hebrews 11:9–10. Suffice it to say that the believer is ultimately a citizen of another world, not this one.

Cass pointed out another important New Testament reference that could be seen as applying to immigrants:

> In one of the most challenging passages in all of Scripture, Jesus makes reference to the "stranger" (Greek: *xenos,* the alien and by implication a guest). "'For I was hungry and you gave Me food; I was thirsty and you gave Me drink; I was a stranger and you took Me in....' And the King will answer and say to them, 'Assuredly, I say to you, inasmuch as you did it to one of the least of these My brethren, you did it to Me'" (Matthew 25:35, 40).
>
> In a most powerful affirmation of the duty of the Christian to "the least of these," Jesus demands that we take a very serious look at our attitude and actions toward the stranger. The duty to the stranger is critical to a thoroughgoing Christian moral framework. But this was not new, per se. It was entirely consistent with the spirit and letter of the Old Testament. We will need to further examine the Old Testament to better understand the radical nature of this moral imperative.

Cass brings to our attention that racism, of sorts, was at work among the temple authorities at that time:

> Racial prejudice and hostility toward the "unwashed" outsiders was common in Israel in Jesus's day. This was apparently built upon an extreme and misguided notion of separation from the

unclean world. But Jesus often made the unlikely outsiders the heroes of his stories. For example, in the account of the ten lepers in Luke 17:18: "Were there not any found who returned to give glory to God except this foreigner?" He was *allogenes,* that is, a foreigner. Some speculate that this was a reference to the hated Samaritans.

Jesus made these objects of extreme prejudice the good guy and portrayed the "righteous" Jews (that is, a certain priest and a certain Levite) as the bad guys. This is most evident in the parable of the Good Samaritan (in Luke 10). It was to a Samaritan *woman* at the well that Jesus made one of the clearest and earliest revelations of Himself as the Messiah (John 4:26). This affirmation of this most despised people is carried on into the apostolic age when Jesus sends out the disciples in Acts 1:8 even to Samaria.

Furthermore, Cass notes that the New Testament commends the church to show hospitality, even to strangers:

> There are four words that are used in relationship to the outsiders in the Old Testament that are translated various ways. Unfortunately, they are not consistently translated, and thus it leads to some confusion. While there is some overlap in their use, we will look at each of them individually and then consider how they were applied in the Old Testament.

CARING FOR THE "STRANGERS" AMONG US

God repeatedly reminds Israel that they were strangers in a strange land (when they were in Egypt), thus they should show mercy to those strangers among them. On the other hand, the strangers (the Gentiles) could not fully participate in temple activities.

Another point of great interest to us is that those strangers (those immigrants, if you will) who learned to acculturate themselves with their adopted land were to be treated favorably. Those who refused to accommodate themselves were to be cut off. In a sense, by their own cultural isolation, they were isolating themselves already.

Here is what Leviticus 19:33–34 says about the stranger (the Hebrew word here is *ger*): "And if a stranger dwells with you in your land, you shall not mistreat him. The stranger who dwells among you shall be to you as one born among you, and you shall love him as yourself; for you were strangers in the land of Egypt: I am the LORD your God."

Furthermore, Cass points out that each of these strangers (ger) were afforded certain rights:

★ Sabbath rest (Exodus 20:10)
★ a fair trial (Deuteronomy 1:16)
★ access to cities of refuge (Numbers 35:15)
★ participation in the feast of booths and weeks (Deuteronomy 16:11, 14)
★ They were guaranteed sustenance by the gleaning laws (Leviticus 19:10) and the triannual poor tithe (Deuteronomy 26:11–12) and the Sabbath-year produce (Leviticus 25:6).
★ The ger was privileged and responsible for observing the Day of Atonement (Leviticus 16:29) and the Passover (Exodus 12:48–49), using unleavened bread (Exodus 12:19), following sacrificial procedures (Leviticus 17:8), following procedures for the purification after eating unclean meat (Leviticus 17:15), not making sacrifices to Molech (Leviticus 20:2), avoiding blasphemy

(Leviticus 24:16), avoiding sexual sin (Leviticus 18:1–26), *lex talionis* (that is, the law of retribution; Leviticus 24:20–22), and circumcision (Exodus 12:43–47).

★ Unclean meat could not be eaten by Israelites, but it might be given to the ger or be sold to foreigners (Deuteronomy 14:21).

★ A ger could even own an Israelite until the year of jubilee (Leviticus 25:47–55).

★ If the nation of Israel broke the covenant, they would be cursed and wind up having to serve the ger (Deuteronomy 28:43).

★ The ger were present when the Law was taught (Deuteronomy 29:10–11) and at covenant renewal (Joshua 8:33). They were not part of David's census (2 Chronicles 2:17), but they were the basis of Solomon's work crews (1 Chronicles 22:2).

★ In the vision of Israel's restored community (Ezekiel 47:22), the identification of the ger with the Israelite community is complete.

Thus, the ger, in essence, were treated like Israelites.

In contrast with the ger is another Hebrew word, *zar* (*zarim*, plural). In the King James Version, this is translated as "stranger." In the Revised Standard Version, it is translated as "stranger," "outsider," "alien," and "foreigner."

★ The root word implies "to turn aside, depart, or deviate."

★ Zar is one outside the household. A widow must not marry a zar if there is another man in the household (Deuteronomy 25:5).

★ Zar was generically applied to the nonpriestly class (Exodus 29:33; 30:33; Leviticus 22:10).

★ The zarim are often seen as creditors who seize the property or consume the produce of another.

- ★ The *zara* are harlots who have deserted their proper place in society and who intrude on another's family. Hosea calls Israel's children the illegitimate sons of zar.
- ★ Fundamentally, zarim are the enemies of a nation and a sign of spiritual adultery.

So we see a distinction in the Old Testament between those strangers who want to follow after God and those strangers who do not. We find those strangers who want to assimilate in their new homeland versus those who will not.

FROM STRANGERS TO IMMIGRANTS

So how do we apply these biblical principles to our current situation? Nick Spencer, a researcher for the Jubilee Center, reminds us that we as Christians need to show love to immigrants: "We need to love the alien in our midst and, in particular, the vulnerable alien, while at the same time stressing the importance of community cohesion and identity. You cannot, after all, welcome the stranger if you have nothing to welcome them into. Having a foot in both camps in this way will invariably open us to hostile criticism from both sides of the debate. That is a perennial danger for the people of the go-between God."[3]

The Roman Catholic Church makes a similar statement. In an article in *Our Sunday Visitor,* Thomas Wenski writes:

Some charge that the church is in favor of a nation without borders, that we support illegal immigration. How do you respond to that?

The church does not favor illegal immigration in any sense. It is not good for the migrant, who often suffers abuse by smugglers,

exploitation in the workplace, and even death in the desert. It is
not good for society or for local communities, because it creates a
permanent underclass with no rights and no opportunity to assert
them. That is why the church supports the creation of legal
avenues for migration and legal status for migrants. The church
has always supported the right of a sovereign nation to secure its
borders, although it should be done in a manner that protects
human life to the greatest degree possible. In any case, the so-called
"illegals" are not the problem and should not be demonized—the
problem that needs to be fixed is the broken system.[4]

PUTTING PRINCIPLES INTO ACTION

Gary Cass says that we should apply these lessons in the following ways:

★ Individuals must show love to individual outsiders as opportunities arise.

★ Families can sponsor outsiders and help them assimilate into the community.

★ Churches must welcome all people and all classes of outsiders, extending mercy in the name of Christ and seeking to evangelize and disciple them. Churches might even offer classes on language and national heritage to assist new immigrants. Of course, this says nothing about what governments should or should not do. (At the least, governments should not impede private charity work, Christian or otherwise, provided such work is legal.)

★ Ancient Israel made a clear distinction between outsiders. Either outsiders were assimilated and received all the rights and duties of citizens, or they were considered foreigners with limited rights and a certain degree of suspicion. Governments have the right to require assimilation and vows of fidelity to the nation and their principles of governance. Governments have the right to enforce their borders; otherwise they cannot enforce or monitor an immigrant's progress in assimilation.

Cass also notes that Christ's genealogy in Matthew, normally used to assert racial purity, goes out of its way to mention two Canaanite women—Tamar and Rahab—Ruth a Moabitess, and Bathsheba, the wife of Uriah, a righteous Hittite.

Finally, there are principles that we need to apply to each sphere of our life:

★ Individually: We must show love practically to strangers (Matthew 25) as well as others.

★ Family: We might need to open our homes as God gives us the grace and opportunity to do so.

★ Church: We must be an example of Christ (Prophet, Priest, and King).

★ Government: "And He has made from one blood every nation of men to dwell on all the face of the earth, and has determined their preappointed times and the boundaries of their dwellings" (Acts 17:26).

In regard to government responsibilities, biblical principles dictate:

1. We must affirm that all men are created equal under God (only one human race).

2. Citizenship ought not be based on ethnicity, economics, etc.—only shared values.

3. Borders are real and useful but not immutable and impermeable.

4. Nations must require affirmation of shared values (oaths, circumcision, e.g., only in the case of Israel).

5. All immigrants have basic human rights and deserve equal protection under the law.

6. Those willing to integrate should be able to share in all the duties of citizens.

Cass also reminds us that we must avoid naive nationalism but appreciate the uniqueness of our national heritage, which in our situation is very much a wonderful Christian heritage.

Meanwhile, there are other considerations as well. We should recognize that there are many illegal aliens who are taking advantage of our way of life. There are many who break the law to come here. We must secure the borders to prevent criminals and potential terrorists from entering our country. These are serious threats. Acting in a Christian way includes concern for self-defense. It is astounding how many crimes are committed by illegal immigrants. To protect ourselves is not un-Christian. We have already seen that war is justified on rare occasions as a last recourse.

Another point, too, is that the Bible seems to distinguish between immigrants who will assimilate versus immigrants who refuse assimilation. It condemns the practice of the latter and commends the former. Whatever laws we adopt, whatever politicians we support, they should move the nation in that direction: helping immigrants to assimilate and, for example, to learn the language.

In the ultimate sense, Christians must see that we, too, are strangers in a strange land. This is not our ultimate home; we are just passing through. Therefore, we should show kindness while still upholding the rule of law. It galls me to see politicians who want to win votes by giving out freebies from the public treasury. When this includes nonpaying noncitizens, the nation will go bankrupt even more quickly than by following the path we are currently taking.

IMMIGRATION REFORM?

In 2007 one of the major political hot potatoes being tossed around was a bill debated in the Senate supposedly promoting immigration reform. Many conservatives said that this bill, crafted largely by Ted Kennedy, would be a costly disaster for the country. In an editorial entitled "Immigration Debacle," the *Washington Times* noted: "It's a disaster for national security, for keeping Islamist Jihadists out of the country, for exploding the costs of Social Security, Medicare and Medicaid, for preserving the rule of law, and for that quaint principle called national sovereignty."[5]

Robert Rector of the Heritage Foundation estimated that American taxpayers would be saddled with a huge bill to pay for the social services needed by all these illegal immigrants for whom this bill would provide amnesty. The immigrants would receive $2.5 trillion more in welfare-type benefits than they would pay in taxes, according to Rector's research.[6] To the superficially minded, this supposedly would make Jesus happy. I'm not so sure. There is a fundamental unfairness to all this.

CONCLUSION

How would Jesus want us to vote on immigration? The short answer is, in a way that would carefully balance these various considerations.

He certainly would want us to be able to protect ourselves. Common sense would prohibit us from allowing everyone to cross our borders, because we know our enemies would love to do us harm. But Jesus would also have us recognize—as individuals and as a church, more than as a nation—that we were once aliens and strangers. Therefore, we should show compassion to the strangers among us.

Not all immigrants are the same. There are those who are willing to acculturate themselves (for example, learn our language) and those who refuse to do so. I am not saying there should be hard-and-fast laws on this (such as requiring only English). But it does not work well for immigrants, for their children, or for our society if they refuse to accommodate their host country in even the simplest ways. Why should they come here if they don't want to have anything to do with us or our way of life?

To say the least, radical jihadists who want to destroy us are not welcome. The hard part is discerning between those who fit in that category versus the Muslims who want to assimilate.

One last consideration is that of social services. Our economy is teetering on bankruptcy because of the rampant abuses of tax-funded social services. How can we possibly pay the bills for the millions of illegal immigrants who want to benefit from our hard-earned social services? Recently I learned that a hospital went out of business because of its proximity to the Mexican border; nonpaying illegal immigrants took advantage of its services. These abuses of our social-services system decrease the quality of life for everyone.

How would Jesus vote on immigration? I think He would want us to consider all the major points in this debate and not simply go with the supposedly obvious solution. The so-called compassionate solution might not be that compassionate after all. And we should make sure that we distinguish between personal ethics and national policy.

Marriage:
Society's Smallest Unit

For the LORD *God of Israel says*
that He hates divorce.

—MALACHI 2:16

Anything good for the family is good for society. Conversely, anything bad for the family is bad for society. It is that simple. When we vote, protecting the sanctity of marriage—society's smallest unit—should be a priority.

Since marriage and the family are ordained by the triune God (who Himself as Father, Son, and Holy Spirit is the model of unity and community simultaneously), we believe it is safe to say that Jesus would have us vote in ways that protect traditional families. Likewise, He would want us to oppose any measures that might work against the family unit.

BEFORE THE STATE, BEFORE THE CHURCH

The oldest institution on this planet is not the state and not the church. It is the institution of marriage, created by God, and the most universal of all of God's institutions. Wherever you might go in this world today, whatever continent, whatever nation, you will find men and women joined in the bonds of matrimony and rearing families.

This is a critical time for marriage as an institution. The *New York Times* declares, "The United States is becoming a post-marital society."[1] Remarkably, in the entire history of the human race, what has happened in just the last few years is a millisecond in the history of mankind.[2] We are seeing a massive effort to destroy that institution—an effort that is making ominously large strides forward.

As far as the biblical record is concerned, God created one man for one woman. So it was in the beginning. It is truly amazing to ponder that God took a part of a man and tailor-made a woman for him. We were made for each other by divine design. That's how it was seen in the Old Testament and in the New Testament.

Christ performed His first miracle at a wedding in Cana of Galilee (see John 2). He defended marriage before the Pharisees, pointing out that when men and women departed from God's design of marriage, it was because of the hardness of their hearts. He said it was not so from the beginning. He brought them back to creation to make His point (see Matthew 19:3–9). Marriage is of historical and biblical importance, and it is basic and essential to the culture in which we live.

THE ASSAULT ON MARRIAGE

This nation was built on a foundation of good families, and that has been the strength of every nation since the beginning of time. Even Napoleon Bonaparte said that what was needed for France to be strong was good mothers—women in families, rearing children. He was a very perceptive man. Strong families are important for a culture. They are important for individuals. They are important for husbands and wives.

But over the last few decades, marriage has been under assault like never before. For example, no-fault divorce laws have made it much easier for people to divorce. The result has been a skyrocketing divorce rate, as well as mountains of evidence showing increased unhappiness. Perhaps no other law has done so much harm to so many people.

I have talked to many people who have said that marriage no longer makes them happy. No-fault laws allow people to say, "I am not happy now. But if I get a divorce, I am going to be happy." The evidence, however, proves that divorce is not a path to happiness.

Studies and books (like *The Case for Marriage* by Linda J. Waite and Maggie Gallagher) have shown that married couples, more than divorced or single people, are generally happier. They have more wealth. On average, they have better homes. They feel their lives are more fulfilling. And they have more fulfilling sex lives than single people (in spite of what virtually every television program depicts). God's way is the right way. Waite and Gallagher state:

> The scientific evidence is now overwhelming: Marriage is not just one of a wide variety of alternate family forms or intimate relations, each of which are equally good at promoting the well-being of children or adults. Marriage is not merely a private taste or a private relation; it is an important public good. As marriage weakens, the costs are borne not only by individual children or families, but also by all of us taxpayers, citizens, and neighbors. We all incur the costs of higher crime, welfare, education and health-care expenditures, and in reduced security for our own marriage investments. Simply as a matter of public health alone, to take just one public consequence of marriage's decline, a new campaign to reduce marriage failure is as important as the campaign to reduce smoking.[3]

Meanwhile, Barbara Dafoe Whitehead chronicled the fallout for children of divorce in her book *The Divorce Culture:*

For parents, divorce is not a solo act, but one that has enormous consequences for children. A mounting body of evidence from diverse and multiple sources shows that divorce has been a primary generator of new forms of inequality, disadvantage, and loss for American children. It has spawned a generation of angry and bereaved children who have a harder time learning, staying in school, and achieving at high levels.... Divorce is never merely an individual lifestyle choice without larger consequences for the society.... It has imposed a new set of burdens and responsibilities on the schools, contributed to the tide of fatherless juveniles filling the courts and jails, and increased the risks of unwed teen parenthood.[4]

More recently, Charles Colson pointed out the devastating consequences of fatherlessness and illegitimacy in our country: "Studies reveal that children without fathers are more likely to grow up in poverty, to have problems in school, to commit crimes. Charles Murray of the American Enterprise Institute wrote that 'illegitimacy is the single most important social problem of our time—more important than crime, drugs, poverty, illiteracy, welfare, or homelessness.' Why? Because illegitimacy 'drives everything else.'"[5]

I am not trying to put a guilt trip on anyone. Some of you may have been divorced. Maybe you were deserted or abandoned, and you are doing the best you can to rear your children. Some of you are doing an outstanding job. Still, children of divorce face staggering problems. They drop out more, get worse grades, get into more trouble, are expelled from school more often, are more likely to take drugs, are likely to drink alcohol more frequently, and commit more crimes while still in school. Children of divorce don't do much better once they reach adulthood.

On average, they get into more crime, make less money, are more unhappy, and, though they despise divorce, are more likely to get one than those who have lived in intact families.

As a matter of compassion, we should care for single parents and the children of divorce. But as a matter of policy, we should support marriage and make divorces harder—not easier—to get.

The Feminist Assault on Marriage

Feminist movement pioneer Betty Friedan likened being a housewife to being in "a comfortable concentration camp."[6] Some feminists abandoned marriage, believing that their fulfillment in life was going to depend on their *not* getting married. But several feminist leaders have realized that their attack on marriage was a failure. Gloria Steinem once said that a woman needs a man like a fish needs a bicycle. Later she married.

The Homosexual Assault on Marriage

A more serious assault has been waged by radical homosexuals who are trying to destroy marriage by redefining it. Throughout history, marriage has been recognized as the union between one man and one woman. Now that tradition is under fire by those who reject biblical teaching.

The Bible condemns the practice of homosexuality, just as it condemns fornication (premarital sex), adultery (sex outside of marriage), incest, and bestiality. In Leviticus 20:13 we read: "If a man lies with a male as with a woman, both of them have committed an abomination; they shall surely be put to death; their blood is upon them" (ESV).[7] In Romans 1:26–28, we read: "For this reason God gave them up to dishonorable passions. For their women exchanged natural relations for those that are contrary to nature; and the men likewise gave up natural relations with women and were consumed with passion for one another, men committing shameless acts with men and receiving in themselves the due penalty for their error. And since they did not see fit to acknowledge God, God gave them up to a debased mind to do what ought not to be done" (ESV). And in 1 Corinthians 6:9–10, we read: "Do not be deceived: Neither the sexually immoral nor idolaters nor adulterers nor male prostitutes nor homosexual offenders [nor others] will inherit the kingdom of God" (NIV).

What should be the attitude of a Christian? We are to love homosexuals while opposing their efforts to redefine marriage. Let me explain. I believe robbery is a terrible sin, and I hate it. I believe rape is a terrible sin, and I hate it. I believe the same thing about murder and many other sins, but that doesn't mean I hate the people who do them. I have counseled people who have done all those things. I have prayed for them, and I have witnessed to them. I don't hate them.

I don't hate homosexuals, nor can you. Let me say this: a study of 1 John makes it abundantly clear that we shouldn't hate anyone. If we say we are children of God, a God who is a God of love, we can't hate people. Vengeance belongs to the Lord, not to us. We are to love sinners, though we hate sin. This has always been my attitude toward homosexuals. But that does not mean we lose all moral discernment and proclaim that what they do is acceptable.

I have counseled many homosexuals. I have known homosexuals who have come out of the homosexual lifestyle. I have known those who are struggling in their efforts to try to overcome homosexuality. I have known those who are in that lifestyle and want to stay there, but I have prayed for every one of them, and so must we all. These are people who are desperately in need of our prayers. Meanwhile, we must be diligent, as Christians, to protect the sanctity of the family when we cast our ballots.

PROTECTING MARRIAGE FROM ASSAULT

Marriage is under assault and in great need of protection. Today three countries recognize same-sex marriage: the Netherlands, Belgium, and Canada. In the United States, the Massachusetts Supreme Court ruled in 2003 that same-sex marriages should be legal. But this legal battle won't stop in Massachusetts. Already homosexuals, through their legal organizations, have filed lawsuits in virtually every state that has passed DOMA (Defense of Marriage Act) laws.[8] The homosexual community is using small groups of unelected officials in the courts (namely, judges) to overthrow an institution that has existed as long as mankind. And they have been amazingly successful.

Why do gays want to get married? For some activist leaders the goal is to destroy marriage altogether.

How would Jesus want us to vote? I believe He would have us oppose any assault on the family.

A COMMITMENT AND A COVENANT

Have you noticed how uncommitted so many millions of people are in our society? Their word is no longer their bond. They break agreements without giving it a thought. The ultimate cause of this is the breaking of so many covenants in marriage (or is it vice versa?). Tens of millions of Americans have forsaken their vows and walked away from the spouse of their youth. Some remarry and remarry and remarry and remarry. Others simply go through a series of live-in lovers or settle into a common-law marriage if a relationship lasts long enough.

The basis for marriage is commitment, a lifetime commitment of one man to one woman and one woman to one man. Marriage is based on a solemn vow: "for better or for worse, for richer, for poorer, in sickness and in health, to love and to cherish, from this day forward until death do us part." Marriage is a commitment that, regardless of what comes, the two promise to work out their problems.

As Christians, we are committed to the fact that divorce is not an option. Unfortunately, that resolve has broken down in our society. It is very important whether a person sees divorce as a possible option or as no option at all. If it is seen as no option at all, it will make a vast difference in the relationship.

But the foundation of marriage is based upon a commitment before God of one man and one woman for life. It is a covenant—a triangular relationship between God, a man, and a woman. Just as the Mayflower Compact was a covenant between God and the signers, holy matrimony is a covenant between God and a husband and a wife. When marriage is only an agreement between two people, they can agree to anything, but a church wedding is so much more. There a third party is involved, namely, God. Therefore, to break a marriage covenant is not only an affront to one's spouse, family, relatives, church, and country, but it is an affront to a covenant-keeping God. Does that mean that divorce is the unforgivable sin? No. However, surely too many Christians today cavalierly disregard their marital vows.

Meanwhile, the state has a vested interest in the quality of our marriages. Obviously that cannot be enforced by the state, but at least the state should not assault traditional marriage by:

1. offering incentives for easy divorce
2. redefining marriage to placate militant homosexuals

3. taxing stay-at-home moms out the door and into the workforce in order to pay more taxes

When we vote, we should keep families as a priority.

A SCOURGE TO THE FAMILY UNIT

We should also combat pornography, including Internet pornography, which is assaulting marriage and sexual morality in ways that no one imagined possible a decade ago. Pornography tears families apart. It leads to fornication (sex before marriage), to adultery, and sometimes to rape. It is harmful to all society. Laws or judicial decisions that tolerate pornography and allow it to flourish are bad for everyone.

We live in a world where lust is rampant. Americans spend approximately $12–13 billion annually on pornography, including videos, magazines, and phone sex.[9]

The Bible has important things to say that protect us by prohibiting sexual sin. For starters, the tenth commandment prohibits lust: "You shall not covet your neighbor's wife" (Exodus 20:17). Lust can easily lead to breaking the seventh commandment: "You shall not commit adultery" (Exodus 20:14).

The word *pornography* has an interesting relationship with adultery. "Porno" means harlot or prostitute. "Graph" means picture. So pornography consists of pictures of prostitutes. Solomon's warnings of not physically going to an adulteress (see Proverbs 5–7) apply as well to not looking at pornography, for in so doing, you could actually be taking the first step toward an adulteress. Furthermore, we read in the Sermon on the Mount: "You have heard that it was said to those of old, 'You shall not commit adultery.' But I say to you that whoever looks at a woman to lust for her has already committed adultery with her in his heart" (Matthew 5:27–28).

Pornography also increases poverty. How? Because the single largest group of poor people in America are the children of single mothers. Many of these partial orphans are indirect victims of fathers who were carried away by pornography. We believe that the laws that discourage pornography are in line with the will of Christ. Laws that promote the distribution of this filth are opposed to His will. Therefore, we need to be careful regarding the judges we choose, the politicians we elect, and the referenda we approve with our vote. (Also, of course, we need to avoid looking at or supporting this destructive material ourselves, lest we join the ranks of the hypocrites.)

CONCLUSION

The family is God's chosen building block of society. Judicial decisions, no-fault divorce laws, and tax burdens that hurt the traditional family hurt all of us. So how would Jesus have us vote? Since He created the family, and since family, in a sense, is a reflection of the community that God the Son has enjoyed for all eternity with God the Father and God the Spirit, He would want us to protect the sanctity of families. Marriage is also a picture of the relationship between Christ and His church.

Personally we need to choose wisely, marry wisely, and live wisely. Politically, we need to vote in ways that protect the sanctity of the family. At the very least, we should oppose those things that would subvert families, like same-sex marriage or pornography or no-fault divorce.

Judicial Activism and the Courts

Hate evil, love good;
Establish justice in the gate.

—AMOS 5:15

One of the great dividing lines between liberals and conservatives today is the judiciary.

How would Jesus vote when it comes to the courts? Of course, it would be a mistake to remake Him into an American constitutionalist. However, it is more than fair to say that American constitutionalism would not have arisen without the fundamental Judeo-Christian ethic He provides.[1]

I believe a case can be made that America is being hijacked by out-of-control judges. Against the will of the people, activists have used the courts to ram their anti-Christian agenda into mainstream America. Abortion, the homosexual agenda, pornography, and many curtailments of religious liberties have been facilitated by court decisions. As former Congressman Henry Hyde once said, the Constitution is like Silly Putty in the hands of a runaway judiciary.[2] Thomas Jefferson, who was not an orthodox Christian but certainly not the rabid secularist he has been remade to be in our time, noted that the Constitution is a "thing of wax" in the hands of some judges.[3] The tragedy is that some of these judges hold their positions for life.

JUDICIAL ACTIVISM

Some said Supreme Court nominee Robert Bork was the most qualified jurist to be nominated to that position in more than a half century.

(The respected, nonpartisan *Oxford Companion to the Supreme Court* notes, "Bork's legal competence and personal integrity were indisputable, and debate focused on his conservative political and legal views."[4]). Bork said recently that "the idea that the Constitution is a 'living document' is really preposterous. What they mean by that is that a judge can change it."[5] By reinterpreting the "living Constitution," the courts have essentially enacted new laws from the bench, amending the Constitution and circumventing public approval.

Judicial activism has become a hot-button issue, with each side in the culture war accusing the other of engaging in it. So what exactly is judicial activism? Best-selling author David Limbaugh defines it well: "Judicial activism is when courts usurp the authority of the legislature. The legislature is the law-making body. Judicial activism is when courts take it upon themselves to make laws, so that instead of adhering to the Constitution's original intent, they rewrite the Constitution or rewrite laws under the Constitution to suit their particular whim or their ideology."[6]

For most of American history, judges have been bound by the wording and intent of a law when ruling. Article 1 of the Constitution, which deals with the legislature, contains 2,266 words. By contrast, article 3, which deals with the judiciary, is only 375 words long. The Founders were more concerned about the legislature than the judiciary, but in recent years, a new philosophy of interpreting laws has arisen.

Robert Knight, a spokesperson for the Media Research Council, noted: "At this point, it's a question of whether we're going to be a self-governing people or not. If the last word is by the judges themselves, and there's no recourse, if legislatures are not willing to override decisions, then the judges in effect rule us—just as kings of old did. This is unacceptable in America."[7]

FAIRNESS AND INVISIBILITY

Consider the role of judges. They are to serve as umpires, invisible to the proceedings of the game. You cannot have a baseball game without an umpire, but you also cannot have a game if an umpire insists on taking an active role in the game. What if an umpire gets drunk on power, and in the middle of a game he decides he wants to have a more active role in the outcome? The result is tainted. This is essentially what is happening in our courts today; many of those who should be adjudicating from the bench are instead legislating from the bench.

Former Reagan administration official Gary Bauer observed: "The fact of the matter is that our courts for a long time now have been sitting as a sort of constant Constitutional Convention, amending our Constitution with each decision. And this is the icing on the cake, the final proof that they are now writing a document that bears no resemblance to the document that our founding fathers gave us and that hundreds of thousands of men have given their lives for."[8]

We should remember what Thomas Jefferson said in 1821: "The germ of dissolution of our federal government is in...the federal judiciary."[9] He also noted a year earlier: "Their power [is] the more dangerous, as they are in office for life and not responsible...to the elective control."[10]

Robert Bork pointed out, "The public is far more conservative than the [Supreme] Court.... The Court is part of the intellectual class and it responds to the intellectual class.... When you [rule] one way, you get praised by all of the *New York Times* and the *Washington Post* and NBC and CBS and ABC; that is kind of seductive. But if you go the other way, you get criticized; and I think that over time, that has some effect on some justices, not all."[11]

Such power as the Supreme Court justices carry cannot help but be seductive for any human being. Judicial activism, where the will of the people is usurped by the courts, is a form of tyranny. America was founded by a people intent on escaping tyrannical rule. Yet today that threat has become commonplace.

Abraham Lincoln addressed the danger of judicial tyranny in his first inaugural address: "If the policy of the government upon vital questions affecting the whole people is to be irrevocably fixed by decision of the Supreme Court...the people will have ceased to be their own rulers."[12]

Has this happened? Columnist and author Wesley J. Smith suggested,

I used to wonder, Why is it that a supposedly liberal judge will very rarely if ever move to the conservative side, but conservative judges often move to the liberal side? And it occurred to me that perhaps the reason for that is: If you're a conservative judge, a so-called strict constructionist, you are pushing away power. You are saying, "It's not up to me to judge, but it's up to a legislature." But if you become a more liberal judge, what you may be saying is, "Hey, I have the power to make that decision." And that can be a very heady seduction, to be able to say, "The law says what I say it says." And perhaps that is why some justices move to the left, but they don't seem to move to the right.[13]

Mat Staver, former pastor, now lawyer (to fight the agenda of the ACLU), noted: "We need to be outraged when Congress doesn't do its job to rein in the Judicial Branch. When the Judicial Branch gets out of control, as it has done for the last many years, then there are ways to rein in that Judicial Branch."[14] As Alexander Hamilton noted in Federalist no. 78,

"The interpretation of the laws is the proper and peculiar province of the courts."[15] In fact, Hamilton added a footnote in which he said, "The celebrated Montesquieu, speaking of them [the branches of government], says: 'Of the three powers above mentioned, the judiciary is next to nothing.'"[16]

THE POLITICIZED PROCESS

It's no secret to those in the know in Washington that the law of the land is in the hands of the courts. This is why the battle over the judiciary has at times been extremely ugly. Some senators send the message to potential appointees that conservative Christians need not apply. Though article 6 of the Constitution specifically prohibits a "religious test" to be applied to anyone in public office, the disturbing current anti-Christian trend very much permeates the judicial nomination process.

When Robert Bork was nominated by Ronald Reagan, he was accused of assaulting the American way of life in every way imaginable. And the attackers later turned their focus on a nominee by George H. W. Bush, Clarence Thomas, who grew up in abject poverty and worked his way up from abysmal conditions to emerge as a conservative African American. When it looked like he was all but a shoo-in to the U.S. Supreme Court, and after a mild grilling at the hands of demagogic senators, suddenly a witness appeared against him: Anita Hill. To this day her accusations of supposed sexual harassment (though nothing like Bill Clinton's proven moral shortcomings) have left a cloud over Thomas's reputation. Many people still believe her story, but most believe him. Thomas declared at the time that he felt this was a "high tech lynching." Ronald Reagan's attorney general, Ed Meese, commented on the travesty against Clarence Thomas: "It's hard to describe how vicious it was. They made up lies about him: they brought in people to tell lies about him—the most vicious kind of lies about his conduct."[17] At the 1991 hearings Thomas said, "My family and I have been done a grave and irreparable injustice."[18]

In the end Gary Bauer observed, "It was an incredible thing to watch those hearings, and of course, at the end of the day, [Thomas] prevailed and is sitting on the Supreme Court, making some decisions that, I think, will have a tremendous lasting impact on our country. The fight over the judiciary may be the most important fight that any president can engage in. A president is [in power], at most, for four or eight years, and then he's gone. But what the courts do, will live on for decades."[19]

CONCLUSION

What does Jesus Christ have to say about the types of judges we should have? The Bible certainly has a lot to say about judges. Most of this is in the Old Testament, but the principles apply just as much today. The overall point is that judges should not be corrupt. They should not take bribes.

Judges hold the power of life and death in their hands since they can sentence individuals to death or decline to commute a death sentence. Therefore, they are a type of god (small *g*). There is, of course, only one God, and He in three persons. However, since a judge has such life-and-death power, the Bible actually calls them "gods" (see Psalm 82:6). Jesus even cited it in a discussion with the Pharisees in John 10 (see verse 34).

I won't say that Jesus would prefer judges who strictly abide by the Constitution. Neither will I say He would oppose all those who would read into the Constitution their own vision of justice. I do think, however, it would be fair to say that Jesus will hold judges accountable, just as He will hold all of us accountable on the Day of Judgment.

Jesus would oppose corrupt judges and those who subvert justice. I believe He wants us to choose judges very carefully—and to consider those who appoint them just as carefully.

May we strive to uphold earthly justice until the day when final justice is served.

Part III

FINAL THOUGHTS

The Problem of Political Compromise

And Elijah came to all the people, and said,
"How long will you falter between two opinions?
If the LORD is God, follow Him;
but if Baal, follow him."
But the people answered him not a word.
—1 KINGS 18:21

After the 2000 election, a conservative black minister from Palm Beach, Florida, asked his congregation, "How many of you are opposed to abortion?" Virtually all hands went up. "How many of you oppose the militant homosexual agenda?" Virtually all hands went up. "How many of you support religious freedom and oppose things like removing God from school?" Virtually all hands went up. "How many of you voted for Al Gore?" Virtually all hands went up.

This minister told this anecdote on Christian radio and made the point that we have a lot of work to do to educate "our people." In this case, he was referring to African Americans. At the present time, the Democratic platform at the national level embraces positions that are contrary to what Jesus has taught us.

Meanwhile, Christian commentator Chuck Baldwin made the point that often the message of many modern Christians is "In the GOP we trust." We are taught to trust God in virtually every realm of our lives, yet when it comes to politics, we are told to put our faith in the Republican Party. However, politicians of any party can generally not be trusted. For every William Wilberforce or George Washington, there are many career politicians whose primary concern is not, "How can I serve my country?" or "How can I serve my Lord?" but rather, "What must I do to get reelected?"

A CONSERVATIVE VICTORY?

In 2006 the Democrats regained control of the House and the Senate, and one of the ways they did that was by running many candidates who were pro-life, pro-family, and pro-God. Keith Thompson, a former liberal, now conservative, noted that the 2006 election was in some ways a victory for conservative values, because without advocating those conservative platforms, the Democrats would not have regained Congress.

Furthermore, Tony Perkins, president of the Family Research Council in Washington, D.C., points to the key reason the Republicans lost in 2006 (in addition to the Iraqi War). The number-one reason cited was the taint of scandal: "While frustration over Iraq helped to oust a 12-year majority, three quarters of the electorate cited corruption as their motivation for sending the GOP packing."[1] The Bible says, "One sinner destroys much good" (Ecclesiastes 9:18).

We are not saying that God is with the Republicans and against the Democrats or vice versa. What we are concerned about is getting the national and local platforms to conform to what the Bible says. Meanwhile, it is up to Christians to show discernment and careful scrutiny before we cast our ballots. It is too easy to put our faith in one political party. But neither party has an exclusive claim to the kingdom of God. Remember when Jesus appeared to Joshua before the battle of Jericho? Joshua asked Him whose side He was on, and Jesus answered, "Neither." The question is not, is God on our side, but rather are we on God's side? Consider the case of a man who did not compromise, even when virtually everyone around him did.

A MOMENTOUS CONFLICT

Examine all of history, sacred and secular, and you will find few, if any, contests comparable to the one between Elijah and the prophets of Baal recounted in 1 Kings 18. Certainly nothing in the Olympics compares with it. There was no victory wreath to be won, but this struggle was a matter of life and death for the people involved and for the nation itself.

Moses and Elijah were the two greats of the Old Testament who appeared with Christ on the Mount of Transfiguration. Moses led the people out from under the oppressive hand of Pharaoh, and at Mount Carmel, Elijah delivered the people of Israel from those who would destroy their faith. Israel had, with the help of God, overcome the armies of Pharaoh; they had destroyed the armies of the Philistines, the Amorites, the Jebusites, and all their other enemies. However, now the struggle was within—the most serious battle of all.

Israel had fallen on hard times. They had an ungodly king and a wicked queen. The nation was infested with priests of an alien religion from Phoenicia, brought to Israel by Queen Jezebel, whose name is now synonymous with evil. Her 450 priests worshiped Baal, the god of the sun and fire, the giver of life, and god of the world, the universe, and nature.

This religion was threatening to crush the religion of Jehovah. It was up to Elijah, one of the few priests of Jehovah left in the world and the only one who was willing to confront the overwhelming numbers of priests arrayed against him. The power of the throne, the power of the false god Baal, and the multitude of the people were all against him.

But Elijah was a man shaped for that hour. He had come to King Ahab three years before, and at the bidding of God, he said, "There shall be no rain in Israel except by my word for these years" (see 1 Kings 17:1). And for three years not a drop of rain fell on the land of Israel or the land of Samaria. The sky had turned to copper. No cloud was seen day after day. Ahab wanted to blame the trouble on the believers, particularly

Elijah. God, who had said to him, "Go, hide yourself" (see 1 Kings 17:3), now said to his prophet, "Go, show yourself" (see 18:1). Elijah emerged from his sequestered life and confronted Ahab. The king gathered up what remaining royal dignity he had left and said to him, "Is that you, O troubler of Israel?" (verse 17).

Elijah, armed with the power of God, replied, "I have not troubled Israel, but you and your father's house have, in that you have forsaken the commandments of the LORD" (verse 18).

CULTURAL ROT

Our days are somewhat similar to those of Elijah. To borrow Rush Limbaugh's term, we have some "cultural rot" going on in America today. John Adams said, "We have no government armed with power capable of contending with human passions unbridled by morality and religion. Avarice, ambition, revenge, or gallantry, would break the strongest cords of our Constitution as a whale goes through a net. Our Constitution was made only for a moral and religious people. It is wholly inadequate to the government of any other."[2] Yet some of our presidents have gone on record as opposing two of the Ten Commandments. Truly America is troubled today:

- ★ We have an epidemic of sexually transmittable diseases with some fifty million carriers of these diseases in America.
- ★ We have a plague of AIDS that is ravaging the land.
- ★ We have crime that is endemic in our streets.
- ★ We have a public education system in rapid decline.

As an alien ideology infiltrates American minds, we face a crisis in America. Yet it is an internal adversary. Abraham Lincoln noted, "If America is ever to be destroyed, it will not come from without, but the destruction will come from within."[3]

We have the priests of humanism, atheism, secularism, and nature worship in our country today. I am certainly in favor of protecting God's world but only as it is the creation of God and not a god itself. America has trouble today, and that trouble is too often being blamed on those who hold to the historic faith.

Elijah did not go to Mount Carmel to present the people of Israel with arguments; they already knew the truth…at least enough of it to cause them to decide. They knew what God had done for them. They knew how God had delivered them with a mighty arm out of the oppression of Egypt, how He had brought them to the Red Sea and the Jordan River and planted them in a Promised Land. They knew how He had protected them from all of their adversaries. Rather Elijah called upon them to decide. Like a sword splitting a rock, he said that the time had come to make a choice: "How long will you falter between two opinions? If the LORD is God, follow Him; but if Baal, follow him" (1 Kings 18:21).

Now Elijah's message does not apply to those who reject Christianity. I am speaking to those who have one foot stuck in the godlessness of this world and the other gingerly in the church, those who love God but embrace political principles clearly spoken against in His Word.

Indecision is the great problem in the church today. Many are determined to serve God and Christ, but they are afraid of missing out on some goodies of this world. They do not want to become too religious, so they have just enough religion to make themselves miserable. Their indecisiveness will be solved at the Final Judgment.

The problem with indecision is that it causes people to do nothing, and that is a great problem in the church. That was the great problem of Elijah's day, and that is why so little progress is made in the kingdom. Like Hamlet's dilemma, millions in the church wonder, *Will I find my greatest happiness and joy here, or will I find my greatest happiness and joy there?* The great tragedy of the indecisive man is that he does nothing at all. God will hold us accountable for everything—including how we vote.

My friend, are you on the fence, mired in the valley of indecision? There are committed Christians around us who take the time to see where the candidates stand on the key issues. We should learn from their research and vote with an informed conscience.

ELIJAH'S TEST

Facing the false prophets of Baal on Mount Carmel, Elijah said, "'If the LORD is God, follow Him; but if Baal, follow him.' But the people answered him not a word" (1 Kings 18:21). These are words and a truth that have broken the heart of many a prophet and many a preacher down through the centuries.

Elijah determined to present a test for the prophets of Baal—a test that would result either in a victory for him and the life of the nation or his destruction and the destruction of the faith of the living God. He called for the prophets and priests of Baal and all of the people of Israel to come to Mount Carmel. There, at the high place for the religion of Baal worshipers, he offered a challenge, to see whose deity would answer a prayer for fire. He gave the priests every opportunity, with the great mass of people as witnesses, to answer his challenge. With their purple robes emblazoned with the symbol of the sun, the priests of Baal accepted the challenge.

Elijah said, "Make an altar. Kill a bull, and call upon Baal, the god of fire, to answer by fire. The God who answers by fire is the true God."

(Incidentally, how many people today would say, "Well, aren't all religions basically the same?")

Early that morning the priests of Baal began to go through their ritual. "O Baal, hear us and answer with fire." They cried until noon, with the sun in the blazing copper sky beating down on them. But there was no answer from heaven. They cried louder. Nothing. At last the afternoon was spent, and the time of the evening sacrifice had come. The priests of Baal gave up in utter defeat.

A palpable stillness came over the people. The wicked king Ahab and the prophets of Baal were there to see if Elijah could do any better. The prophet took twelve large stones and rebuilt the altar of Jehovah that had previously stood on this place. Then he put wood on it, and the bull was cut and placed on that. Next Elijah dug a trench around the altar and ordered four barrels of water poured into it. Then he called for four more barrels and four more, until the trench was filled with water. Elijah stepped forward, lifted his face to heaven, and said, "LORD God of Abraham, Isaac, and Israel, let it be known this day that You are God in Israel and I am Your servant, and that I have done all these things at Your word" (verse 36).

Suddenly out of the cloudless sky there came a streak of fire blazing from the heavens, striking the altar, consuming the bull, consuming the wood, consuming the stones, and licking up the very water in the trench. The people were so astonished they fell on their faces and cried out at the top of their voices: "The LORD, He is God! The LORD, He is God!" (verse 39). The sound of their shouts rang from the mountains around them. Finally a decision had been wrenched from them.

THE FIRE OF GOD'S WRATH

Now, today, we are not likely to see such fire descend from heaven, and we don't need it to, for that fire has already come, and God does not choose to demonstrate Himself in such fashion for every generation throughout the world. On another mountain covered with blood, on the black hill of Calvary, the altar was prepared, and the wood was set in place, and the Son of God was skewered. The fire of God's wrath for sin fell upon Him who bore in His own body and soul the guilt of our sin, and the wrath of God consumed all of that guilt and all of that sin and all of that iniquity.

We need no demonstration today. We know what Christ has done. We know the price He paid. We know the gospel. We know that "God so loved the world that He gave His only begotten Son, that whoever believes in Him should not perish but have everlasting life" (John 3:16). We know the marvelous offer that eternal life is free to those who will repent of their sins and receive Christ as Lord and Savior. Therefore, what is needed is not argumentation but a decision. Choose you this day…if the Lord is God, follow Him, but if Baal, follow him…but get off the fence.

In the book of Revelation, Jesus tells us that He will spit out those who are neither hot or cold. That is to say, my friend—and this is shocking to contemplate—but some of us make Jesus nauseous…the lukewarm ones, those who are neither hot nor cold. Sad to say, that makes up a good portion of our churches in America.

Will you decide? Will you get off the fence? Christ says, "I would rather that you were either hot or cold" (see Revelation 3:15). He would prefer you were cold rather than lukewarm.

CONCLUSION

America needs a prophet—a prophet who has the ear of America and will say to her now, "How long will you falter between two opinions? If the LORD is God, follow Him; but if Baal, follow him."

I pray that God helps us get off our fences. I pray that the Lord helps us to plant both feet in the kingdom of God and determine with our heart and mind and body and soul that we shall serve the King of kings. I pray that He would help us to meet the crisis of our time—a crisis perhaps more dangerous than the crisis of nuclear bombs, a crisis that threatens to destroy not merely our lives and bodies but our everlasting souls. I pray that He would help us see the signs of the times and rise to the great issues before us and stop our deadly compromises.

Those deadly compromises are seen so often when Christians cast a ballot in a way that has no connection to their faith. We will give an account for every aspect of our lives, including how we vote. May the Lord give us wisdom to obey Him in this as well as in all areas of our lives.

Put Not Your Trust in Princes

Thus says the LORD: "Cursed is the man
who trusts in man
and makes flesh his strength,
whose heart departs from the LORD."

—JEREMIAH 17:5

It is so easy to put our trust in politicians rather than in God. In my opinion, the best president of my lifetime was Ronald Wilson Reagan, the fortieth individual to hold that office. On the eve of his presidency, I warned my congregation that while this was great news (that he was president), we ought not to put our trust in Reagan but in the Lord. I trust that Reagan himself would have agreed with my message. Here is a portion of that message I delivered on January 25, 1981, when the nation had high hopes:

> The events of the recent past have brought a certain euphoria to America, filling a vast number of people in this country with a sense of expectation that things are going to be better in this land. One hears such things as: "I surely hope Ronald Reagan can do something to turn this country around," or, "I trust that he is going to shore up our crumbling defenses in the face of the increasingly menacing Soviet threat." Also, "I certainly trust that he will do something to change the economy." All of which, along with countless other questions, expressed or unexpressed in the minds of many, raise this bottom-line question: Can Ronald Reagan save America?[1]

I went on to say that Reagan was great and he would likely be a tool for positive change but that he was only a man, and we should put our trust in God.

This question brings into focus one of the most important issues facing us in the great controversy across America today, the great struggle of which many people are not even aware. It is the struggle between secular humanism and Christianity, which today are locked in battle in this nation.

There has always been a struggle between faith and unbelief, which is the only real struggle worthy of one's attention, as one great historian put it. The Bible answers that question for us clearly: "Cursed is the man who trusts in man and makes flesh his strength, whose heart departs from the LORD" (Jeremiah 17:5). The Bible tells us also: "Do not put your trust in princes, nor in a son of man, in whom there is no help. His spirit departs, he returns to his earth" (Psalm 146:3–4). We are told instead, "Blessed is the man who trusts in the LORD, and whose hope is the LORD" (Jeremiah 17:7).

So here are the two basic views of life, or laws of life, that are seen everywhere in this discussion: trust in the living God versus trust in man. The Bible says that those who trust in man will be like a withered shrub growing in the desert, in the parched and salted land, where there is no rain or dew, and they shall not even see nor experience the good when it comes (see Jeremiah 17:5–6).

But those who trust in the Lord will be like a tree planted by rivers of water, their roots spread out and drawing nourishment. It shall not feel when the heat comes, and when the drought comes, it shall not even know, because the blessing of God will be upon it (see Psalm 1:1–3).

Returning to what I said in 1981, I pointed out that some were trusting in man (Reagan), not God:

How different are the results described for those who trust in God and those who trust in man. I am afraid some of us, though loudly proclaiming ourselves to be Christians, are at least partial humanists. That is, we trust Jesus Christ to save our souls, but we trust President Reagan to save our country. This is seen, if you would be honest, in the fact that there is less prayer, less witness, less work, less giving, and less trust in the Lord for the country, because many people feel that a man on a white horse has arrived and is going to take care of us. This, according to the Scripture, is a very dangerous attitude.[2]

If you are seasoned enough to remember the 1950s, the same sort of euphoria came over the country then. There was a strong man in the White House who was able to take care of America. We did not need to worry about an overseas threat. All was going to be well, and there was great nominalism in the church—a lot of form and little substance. What happened? People turned the running of the government over to men, prayers decreased, and it gave rise to the decade of the 1960s, where we had virtual rebellion and almost anarchy on every side. It was a time of unbridled unbelief, and the "God is dead" era came upon us.

There is a great danger in victory. Many people survive defeat much better than they survive victory, because defeat turns their hearts toward the Lord, and victory so often turns our hearts away from Him. There are temptations in victory: to pride instead of genuine thankfulness to God, to haughtiness instead of humility, to apathy instead of continued and eternal vigilance, to trusting in men instead of God. After victory many people give up the struggle and later discover they had won only a battle, not the war. Are you working less, praying less, giving less, trusting less? Maybe there is a bit of humanist in all of us.

What we need, however, has not changed. We need a genuine revival in this country. We need to see tens of millions of people swept into the kingdom of God. We need to see the gospel of Jesus Christ proclaimed like never before. Only this is going to avert the judgment of God upon this nation.

What I said in 1981 still holds true: "Right now we have a brief respite, but the question is, what are we going to do with it? Are we going to rest upon our laurels? Are we going to sit back and simply relax, or are we going to pray and work harder than before?"[3]

GOOD VS. EVIL

There is a great biblical example of the truth expressed in 1 Samuel 17, relating an encounter between a prince-to-be and a formidable foe. I am referring to the familiar story of David and Goliath. This story is so familiar that people often miss its deepest spiritual truth.

You recall the incident. The Philistine army had been drawn up on one mountain, and on the mountain on the other side of the Valley of Elah was the army of Israel. The Philistines sent out a champion, Goliath of Gath, who indeed was a remarkable man. We may not understand how long cubits and spans are, but to give you some idea, he was about two and a half feet taller than Wilt Chamberlain. Now, that is a giant! I venture to say he would have weighed close to 400 pounds (and most of that was pure muscle). With his armor, which weighed 150 pounds, he would be a 550-pound man. The head of his spear weighed 18 pounds, which is about the weight of a bowling ball. He was indeed an imposing sight. He was the original "Incredible Hulk," except that he would have taken that little green man and flicked him away.

For forty days this great giant of Gath had come forth and mocked the Israelites, blasphemed their God, and challenged them to come fight him. If the Philistines were defeated, they would forever serve the Israelites, and vice versa. The Israelites cowered in their trenches at the sight of the gigantic man. Then a series of "coincidental" events occurred.

But these events were entirely providential, the outworking of the sovereign hand of God. When one thinks about what happened, one realizes how great is our God who was preparing David for the throne.

Jesse had taken his youngest son, David, from tending the flocks and sent him with food to his three older brothers, who were in the army of Saul. David came to the Valley of Elah, which was about ten miles from Bethlehem, greeted his brothers, and gave them the food.

About that time, to David's astonishment, there emerged from the ranks of the other side this gigantic hulk of a man. He began to blaspheme the God of Israel and mock the soldiers of Saul. David said, "What shall be done for the man who kills this Philistine and takes away the reproach from Israel? For who is this uncircumcised Philistine, that he should defy the armies of the living God?" (1 Samuel 17:26). David's brothers looked at him as if he had lost his mind.

David said that if no one else would go, he would fight the giant. This rumor was passed on to Saul, who summoned the shepherd boy. Saul was astonished to find that David was only a stripling, a young man, a child, and he said:

"You are not able to go against this Philistine to fight with him; for you are a youth, and he a man of war from his youth."

But David said to Saul, "Your servant used to keep his father's sheep, and when a lion or a bear came and took a lamb out of the flock, I went out after it and struck it, and delivered the lamb from its mouth; and when it arose against me, I caught it by its beard, and struck and killed it. Your servant has killed both lion and bear.... The LORD, who delivered me from the paw of the lion and from the paw of the bear, He will deliver me from the hand of this Philistine." (verses 33–37)

So Saul determined to let him fight Goliath. Saul gave David his armor to wear, but it was far too big. David insisted on not using it. Instead, he took in one hand his shepherd's staff and in the other hand his sling. He then went to a stream and picked out five smooth stones, which he placed in his shepherd's bag. When the giant, who was seated in front of the Philistine troops, saw this young boy coming toward him, he was utterly outraged and indignantly said, "Am I a dog, that you come to me with sticks?... I will give your flesh to the birds of the air and the beasts of the field!" (verses 43–44).

David responded with these memorable lines: "You come to me with a sword, with a spear, and with a javelin. But I come to you in the name of the LORD of hosts, the God of the armies of Israel, whom you have defied. This day the LORD will deliver you into my hand" (verses 45–46).

Instead of cautiously watching the giant's moves, David set out at a run, full speed ahead, right at the giant. As he did so, he placed one of the stones in his sling, whirled it around his head, and flung it.

Now consider that this giant was covered with armor from head to foot, except for one small place in his face and a portion of his forehead. The shot stone sank into his forehead, between his eyes, and the giant collapsed with a great tremor upon the earth. David dashed up and took Goliath's own sword and cut off the giant's head.

Did the Philistines do as they had promised? Did they give themselves over to Israel to be their servants forever? Do not ever believe the word of an unbeliever. They fled, every man as fast as he could back to their homeland, with the armies of Israel in hot pursuit.

The lesson here applies not to the situation that we face in our country today but to a thousand other situations that every one of us face every day. David trusted in the living God. He said, "I come to you in the name of the LORD of hosts." He trusted in the Lord—not in anything that he himself could do. That was the secret of his strength. He had not self-confidence but God-confidence. While there were many self-confident Israelites cowering in the trenches, this man of God with a genuine faith and confidence in his Lord was the only one who was not afraid.

On the other hand, you will notice that David had carefully made and measured that sling. He particularly chose five smooth stones of just the right size. It is without question that David had, for many hours and many days and many years, practiced the art of the sling. How many trees in Bethlehem bore the evidence of the practice of the eye and hand of young David?

But he did not trust in his sling. He did not trust in his arm. He did not trust in his skill. He did not trust in the stone. He trusted in God.

We seem to go to one extreme or the other. There are those who say we are to trust in God. What they mean is we should not do something that common sense indicates we ought to do. So we trust in God and do nothing. At the other extreme, we say, "Well, it is all up to us, and God helps those who help themselves." My friend, this is just not true. God helps those who trust in *Him* and then make use of the proper means. There are many who trust in their own efforts. They have nervous breakdowns because they are trusting in their own skills, their own abilities, their own techniques, and they just cannot make them work.

David used the means, which were carefully selected, but he trusted in God, and the difference is the difference between blessing and cursing. It is the difference in human lives between a withered shrub planted in the salt-laden wilderness of the desert and a luxuriant tree planted beside a river.

Back in 1981, I reminded my congregation and the broadcast audience shortly after Reagan's first inauguration:

> Every one of us faces these temptations over and over again. Right now, we face them as a nation. Ronald Reagan is but a means; the government of this country is the government of the people, and the people are using that government to accomplish certain ends. As he himself said in his inaugural speech, "There are some governments that have nations, but this is a nation that has a government." That government is a means and should be a means to godly ends. Ronald Reagan is but a stone in the sling, and you do not trust in stones; you trust in the living rock, Jesus Christ.[4]

We all face giants in our own life, in our home life, in our business, in school, in personal relationships, in our health. Certainly, we ought to make use of what our God-given intelligence tells us in accordance with His Word. Yet we do not trust in the tools but in the living God.

TRUST IN GOD

"Cursed is the man who trusts in man" (Jeremiah 17:5). This is never more true than when it comes to our eternal salvation. There is always and everywhere a universal temptation to trust in man, to trust in the arm of flesh, to trust in self, to trust in our own ability, to trust in our own piety, to trust in our own character, to trust in our own morality, to trust in our own performance, rather than to trust in the living God.

"Blessed is the man who trusts in the LORD, and whose hope is the LORD" (Jeremiah 17:7). David provides an excellent example of this great truth, because he is a genuine type of Christ. You may notice the parallels:

★ Before David came to Elah, he was anointed by Samuel to be king. Before Jesus started His ministry, He was anointed by the Holy Spirit to be King forever.

★ As David was a shepherd, Jesus is our Good Shepherd.

★ As David had been sent by his father to his brethren to minister to them, so Jesus was sent by His Father to minister to us.

★ When David came, he was treated contemptuously by his brothers; so Jesus was mocked and spat upon by those to whom He came. And yet, like David, He did not return their reviling.

★ David was told that his reward would be the king's daughter in marriage. Jesus earned the King's daughter as well, and that, my friend, is His church. We are the spouse of Christ. And for our sake He went forth and faced the Evil One, of whom Goliath is but a mere shadow.

★ Jesus destroyed Satan with His own unlikely weapon.

★ Goliath was a champion, but the Hebrew word used in this passage translates as "middleman" or "representative." David was the middleman for Israel, and Jesus is the middleman for God and us. As David saved God's ancient people, Israel, so Jesus saves the Israel of God today, providing that we trust Him.

"Cursed is the man who trusts in man and makes flesh his strength.... [But] blessed is the man who trusts in the LORD" (Jeremiah 17:5, 7). Blessed is he who trusts in the Lord Christ, Jehovah Jesus, who came to enter into that great battle with Satan. There on the cross, that lion out of hell, sprang upon Christ, and Christ bore all the fangs of that beast, destroyed him, and conquered death. If we trust Jesus for our salvation, shall we not also trust Him to guide us to be good citizens as well?

NATIONAL DAYS OF PRAYER DURING THE REVOLUTION

Thus, we must trust God and not the efforts of men. I like the statement that we should pray as if it all depends on God but work as if it all depends on us.

Because so much of this book is geared to an American audience, I want to remind our readers of the importance of Christianity in the founding of the nation, wherein we were given the freedom to participate in our government in the first place. Voting is the simplest act of such participation.

The settlers and the founders of this nation certainly believed prayer was important. Do you know how many times Congress called for national days of prayer, humiliation, and fasting during the American Revolution?

David Barton is a walking encyclopedia on the Christian roots of America. During an interview for Coral Ridge Ministries about the colonial days of prayer, he said: "Throughout the Continental Congress, or the period of the Continental Congress, which is prior to the Revolution, during the Revolution, and up to the Constitution, you'll find that the Congress called for fifteen nationwide days of prayer and fasting, or days of prayer and thanksgiving.... And that's a tradition that was deeply rooted in America. Between 1633 and 1812, there were over 1,700 prayer proclamations issued in the colonies, where the governor would call the state to an annual day of prayer and fasting, annual day of prayer and thanksgiving."[5]

These days of fasting and prayer and thanksgiving were not like some of today's political prayers, which could just as well be addressed "To whom it may concern." On July 13, 1775, Connecticut governor Jonathan Trumbull wrote to Gen. George Washington, telling him of a congressional call for prayer:

> The Honorable Congress have proclaimed a Fast to be observed by the inhabitants of all the English Colonies on this continent, to stand before the Lord in one day, with public humiliation, fasting, and prayer, to deplore our many sins, to offer up our joint supplications to God, for forgiveness, and for his merciful interposition for us in this day of unnatural darkness and distress.
>
> They have, with one united voice, appointed you to the high station you possess. The Supreme Director of all events hath caused a wonderful union of hearts and counsels to subsist among us. Now therefore, be strong and very courageous.
>
> May the God of the armies of Israel shower down the blessings of his Divine Providence on you, give you wisdom and fortitude, cover your head in the day of battle and danger, add success, convince our enemies of their mistaken measures, and that all their attempts to deprive these Colonies of their inestimable constitutional rights and liberties are injurious and vain.[6]

Note the biblical allusions that Trumbull assumed (correctly) his hearer would understand. Thankfully, God answered those prayers.

Consider the example of John Hancock's proclamation of 1791, long after God granted victory to the American cause. When Hancock was governor of Massachusetts, he proclaimed a statewide day of thanksgiving and prayer. He thanked the Lord for all His blessings, and he encouraged his hearers to thank God for one blessing after another:

> And above all, not only to continue to us the enjoyment of our civil Rights and Liberties; but the great and most important Blessing, the Gospel of Jesus Christ: And together with our cordial acknowledgments, I do earnestly recommend, that we may join the penitent confession of our Sins, and implore the further continuance of the Divine Protection, and Blessings of Heaven upon this People; especially that He would be graciously pleased to direct, and prosper the Administration of the Federal Government, and of this, and the other States in the Union— To afford His further Smiles on our Agriculture and Fisheries, Commerce and Manufactures—To prosper our University and all Seminaries of Learning—To bless the Allies of the United States, and to afford His Almighty Aid to all People, who are virtuously struggling for the Rights of Men—so that universal Happiness may be established in the World; that all may bow to the Scepter of our LORD JESUS CHRIST, and the whole Earth be filled with His Glory.[7]

Note the emphasis in the original. Hancock points to Jesus Christ, the true King of kings. Those who think our Founding Fathers were just deists should sit up and read this proclamation (and other colonial proclamations as well). There are many Christians today who believe that Christians should have nothing to do with politics. I am very thankful that the Founding Fathers did not feel that way. We would not enjoy the freedoms we do if they had felt differently.

A STERN WARNING

My friend Rabbi Daniel Lapin offered this stern warning, addressed to you and all committed Christians who do not want to see our country sink further into the abyss:

> Without a vibrant and vital Christianity, America is doomed, and without America, the West is doomed.
>
> Which is why I, an Orthodox Jewish rabbi, devoted to Jewish survival, the Torah and Israel am so terrified of American Christianity caving in.
>
> Many of us Jews are ready to stand with you. But you must lead. You must replace your timidity with nerve and your diffidence with daring and determination. You are under attack. Now is the time to resist it.[8]

I could not agree more. Now is the time, dear friend.

CONCLUSION

God created only one country in the history of the world: ancient Israel. He did not create America. The United States is not the new Israel. The United States is not now nor ever was a theocracy, although the Puritans attempted to create such a colony in Massachusetts. That attempt failed, but because they culled the Word of God for biblical principles on government, law, civil liberties, education, and morality, the Puritans have essentially served as the midwives of our current freedoms.

We do not claim that God is on the side of the United States. What we do claim is that as many people as possible in the United States should strive to be on God's side. Abraham Lincoln put it best in 1863 when he heard someone remark that he hoped "the Lord was on the Union's side." Here is how Lincoln responded: "I am not at all concerned about that, for I know that the Lord is always on the side of the right. But it is my constant anxiety and prayer that I and this nation should be on the Lord's side."[9]

I believe this is the same attitude with which we should approach the ballot box—to glorify God in all things, even how we vote.

Something More Basic Than Politics

*For by grace you have been saved
through faith, and that not of yourselves;
it is the gift of God,
not of works, lest anyone should boast.
For we are His workmanship,
created in Christ Jesus for good works,
which God prepared beforehand
that we should walk in them.*
—Ephesians 2:8–10

We opened this book noting there are some things the gospel can do that politics cannot. Perchance there is a reader who does not know the gospel. Let me explain it in a nutshell.

Suppose you were to die today and were to stand before almighty God, and He were to say to you, "What right do you have to enter into My heaven?" What would you say? That was a question I had never even thought about when I was a young man. But in my early twenties, I heard that question on the radio on a Sunday, and I was troubled by it—because I did not have an answer. Since we are all going to die, we must be prepared.

I found a copy of Fulton Oursler's *The Greatest Story Ever Told.* I read it that week, finishing it on a Saturday night. Having completed that book, I slipped out of my chair onto my knees and invited Christ into my life, and my life was changed. I didn't have a vision; I didn't hear an angelic choir. I simply prayed, "Lord, I didn't know. I didn't understand. I'm sorry, Lord. Forgive me."

The next morning as I was shaving, I realized that if I were to die that day, I would be in heaven forever in Christ, and a chill went down my spine. That is the greatest thought I have ever had in my life. I was changed that day and became a new person.

Prior to my coming to faith in Jesus Christ, my answer to that question (why should God let me into heaven?) was completely wrong. I had formerly said, "I've tried to live a good life and follow the Ten Commandments and obey the Golden Rule." However, the truth of the matter is I had succeeded at none of those things, and neither has anyone else. We have all fallen short. The most amazing discovery of my life was that heaven, paradise forever and ever, is unearned, unmerited, undeserved, unachievable. It is an absolutely free gift.

Do you have that gift? If you have it, you know it. If you answered the question the way I did prior to my coming to faith—that you have done this or that or the other thing—if Christ is not the person you are trusting in for your hope of eternal life, then you have no hope at all.

I urge you to invite Him into your heart, to place your trust in Christ alone for your salvation. Then you will know beyond any doubt that you are going to be with Him forever in heaven. Christ has said, "He who believes in Me has everlasting life" (John 6:47).

Would you like to trust Him? Would you like to invite Him into your heart and receive Him as Lord and Savior of your life? If so, bow your head and pray with me this prayer right now.

Lord Jesus Christ, divine Savior, Son of God, come into my life I pray right now. I invite You to take over my life. I place my trust in You. I believe that You died in my place and paid the penalty for my sins. I surrender myself to You. I thank You for giving me the gift right now of everlasting life. Help me henceforth to follow You and to turn from my sins and all my wrongdoings and to follow Your law. In Your name. Amen.

I hope, dear friend, that you prayed that prayer just now. If so, that is the most important prayer you have ever prayed in your life. I want to give you something that will help you as you begin your new life with Christ. I have written a book entitled *Beginning Again,* which is what you are doing right now. It will tell you how to grow in your Christian life, how to read the Bible and understand it,[1] how to pray, how to share this faith with loved ones and friends, and how to find a Christ-centered church.[2] I believe it will be a big help to you, so I would like to ask you to call or write today and ask for a copy of *Beginning Again.*[3]

God bless you as you do.

Soli Deo Gloria

Defending Religious Liberty

Where the Spirit of the Lord is,
there is liberty.

—2 CORINTHIANS 3:17

I believe that Jesus Christ promotes freedom. Wherever people truly follow Him by applying the simple gospel, freedom follows—eventually even freedom for those who are not believers. Jesus is for religious liberty. Yet He does not force His way. Secular fundamentalism, the dominant view of the cultural elite, is a jealous faith and cannot countenance opposition. So, in America today, a country founded in large part for religious liberty, we have precious little left of that commodity. I believe Jesus would have us vote in a way that promotes religious liberty.

The Lord warned us about opposition to His message. The Bible says, "The king's heart is in the hand of the LORD... He turns it wherever He wishes" (Proverbs 21:1). God chose to use Caesar to bring about the prophecy written five hundred years before. But, we read, "There was no room for them [Mary and Joseph] in the inn" (Luke 2:7). They were turned away. Our nation's birth certificate declares our rights to come from God and that our government's role is to acknowledge those rights; if it does not, the government is illegitimate. Tragically, today there is increasingly no room in this country for Christ.

There is no room in our inn. There is no room in our cities or parks. There is no room in the cemetery near Pearl Harbor when a man says he was "offended" by the thousands of white crosses. A court ruled in his favor, and the crosses were removed.

There is no room in many businesses or homes. Even at Christmastime. How many office parties take pains not to mention the reason for the season? Can you imagine a birthday party in your honor where no one pays attention to you or mentions your name? Of the four billion Christmas cards sent out last year in America, the vast majority had nothing to say about Christ.

But even that doesn't indicate how ridiculous the anti-Christian sentiment gets. Recently children at the Ridgeway Elementary School in Dodgeville, Wisconsin, performing in a "winter program," were to sing "Silent Night" with the words "Cold in the night, no one in sight, winter winds whirl and bite, how I wish I were happy and warm, safe with my family out of the storm."[1]

You may have noticed seeing the letters CE rather than AD with dates. Rather than "in the year of our Lord," many refer to the "common era."

No room.

In C. S. Lewis's *The Lion, the Witch, and the Wardrobe,* the white witch made the fantasy land of Narnia "always winter, but never Christmas." That is, until Aslan came to reverse the spell. Secularists today are doing the white witch's work for her.

Even the Unitarian-leaning Thomas Jefferson[2] appealed to Jesus Christ ("the holy author of our religion") and His example as to how it is we have religious freedom. In 1786 Jefferson wrote: "Almighty God hath created the mind free, and…all attempts to influence it by temporal punishments…are a departure from the plan of the holy author of our religion, who being lord both of body and mind, yet [chose] not to propagate it by coercions on either, as was in his Almighty power to do, but to exalt it by its influence on reason alone."[3] Thus, according to Jefferson, Jesus is the ultimate source of our liberty.

Bill Federer compiled a classic one-volume encyclopedia of quotes from the settlers and founders of our nation, *America's God and Country.* He noted:

> Tolerance was an American Christian contribution to the world. Just as you drop a pebble in the pond, the ripples go out, there was tolerance first for Puritans and then Protestants, then Catholics, then liberal Christians, and then it went out completely to Jews. Then in the early 1900s, tolerance went out to anybody of any faith, monotheist or polytheist. Finally, within the last generation, tolerance went out to the atheist, the secular humanist and the antireligious. And the last ones in the boat decided it was too crowded and decided to push the first ones out. So now we have a unique situation in America, where everybody's tolerated except the ones who came up with the idea. And so when people say Christians are intolerant, we really need to correct them and say, "No, we're the ones who came up with the idea of tolerance."[4]

Take a look at some of the recent crises that the Christian Law Association of Seminole, Florida (David Gibbs II and David Gibbs III and associates), have contended with:

★ A group of public-school students in Illinois were told they would be expelled if they talked about Jesus in school.

★ A teacher at a public high school in Texas asked students to use scientific steps to prove the falsity of the biblical claim that Moses parted the Red Sea.

★ School officials in West Virginia placed a public-school student in detention because she brought her Bible to school.

★ A student in Kentucky was told she could not place a Ten Commandments poster on her public-school locker.

★ A Christian student in North Carolina was told he could not read his Bible, a book about the Constitution and Christian values, or even a Christian magazine at his public school.

★ University students in Indiana were prohibited from mentioning Jesus by name in an advertisement for their Christian group, while the messages of secular groups go uncensored.

★ A Christian club on a New York college campus was told that their group could not meet unless they agreed that non-Christians could have voting memberships and serve in the club leadership, while other clubs are permitted to restrict leadership to students who share their objectives.[5]

These seem like extreme cases of intolerance. Yet the reality is that these instances are not unique. They happen all the time.

In fact, on January 19, 2007, in Key Largo, two Gideons (the Bible folks) were arrested for handing out Bibles on a public sidewalk. WorldNetDaily.com noted:

Officials with the Alliance Defense Fund have confirmed they will be representing Anthony Mirto and Ernest Simpson, who were arrested, booked into jail and charged with trespassing....

"Neither man entered school grounds," the law firm said. "After the school's principal called police, a Monroe County sheriff's officer asked the men to leave immediately or face trespassing charges. As the men prepared to leave, the officer decided to arrest both individuals."[6]

On and on it goes, despite the unconstitutionality of assaulting religious liberty.

THE AMERICAN CIVIL LIBERTIES UNION

The American Civil Liberties Union (ACLU) began the anti-Christian crusade that drives many of these lawsuits. Radical from the beginning, the ACLU continues to project a radical stance, attempting to remake America into a nation our founders would never recognize. When religious liberty disappears, other liberties will follow. Despite the fact that the Founders said that religion and morality are the twin pillars upon which government rests and that no one should claim to be a patriot who would labor to undermine those pillars, that is exactly what is happening today. The ACLU forbids you to put a nativity scene or a cross on public property.

The ACLU once fought to have a Christmas tree removed from a town square because they found a single ornament with a cross inside. Considering the tax-dollar-supported painting of Christ on a cross submerged in a pot of urine, someone noted that if the ornament had been submerged in that way, the ACLU would have had no objection.

The greatest threat to religious liberty in America began with an organization that claims to be as American as apple pie, but in reality the ACLU has always been hostile to the Founders' vision of one nation under God. I call it "the Anti-Christian Litigation Unit."

Many people don't realize how radical the ACLU is. In 1920 this organization began with a very different vision for America than that of our Founding Fathers. The founder was a Unitarian from Boston, Roger Baldwin, who was a believer in what the godless Soviet Union was attempting to do. He wrote *Liberty Under the Soviets,* defending notorious dictator Josef Stalin. Baldwin stated: "Repressions in Western democracies are violations of professed constitutional liberties, and I condemn them as such. Repressions in Soviet Russia are weapons of struggle in a transition period to socialism."[7]

William Donohue, head of the Catholic League, has written a major book on the ACLU: *Twilight of Liberty.* In an interview he said:

When the ACLU was founded in 1920, it had a group of people who were associated with the far left. In fact, it had a number of people who were proud to call themselves card-carrying members of the Communist party in this country....

The ACLU was not a Communist front to the extent that it was on Moscow's payroll or that it took its directives from Moscow. It would be accurate to say, however, that in the 1920s and 30s, the ACLU had a number of active Communists in its ranks in the senior leadership positions and was persuadable by these people.[8]

But knowing that would not play well with most Americans, ACLU founder, Roger Baldwin, resorted to subterfuge. He wrote to a colleague:

We want also to look like patriots in everything we do. We want to get a good lot of flags, talk a good deal about the Constitution and what our forefathers wanted to make of this country, and to show that we are really the folks that really stand for the spirit of our institutions.[9]

Attorney Herb Titus was once an active member of the ACLU—until he became a born-again Christian. He pointed out the overall motivation of the ACLU on religion and other matters from firsthand experience:

> In the 1960s there was a definite plan to rid this nation of all public displays of any religious symbol of this nation's founding. That's been going on for over fifty years and it will continue....
>
> Well, the ACLU is an organization that is dedicated to changing America: to make America a socialist country: to make America a country that resembles the Soviet Union, or the old Soviet Union, or other communist countries. That's what the ACLU has been about from the very beginning.[10]

Article 52 of the Soviet Union's constitution stated: "The church in the USSR shall be separated from the state and the school from the church." Sound familiar? Here is the origin of the "separation of church and state" the ACLU argues that America's founders intended. Though the Founding Fathers intended there be no national denomination, in the First Amendment they declared, "Congress shall make no law respecting an establishment of religion or prohibiting the free exercise thereof."

Free exercise. Is that what we have?

For the first 150 years after those words were ratified, they were understood to mean there would be no national church. Indeed, for many years after the Bill of Rights was adopted, several individual states maintained their own state churches. However, the ACLU argued in the 1940s that the Founders intended a complete separation between the government and anything religious. When ACLU attorneys in 1947 persuaded the Supreme Court to ignore history and suddenly agree with them on a complete separation of church and state, it was only a matter of time before public expressions of religion—including school prayer and Bible reading and posting the Ten Commandments on courtroom walls—would be declared unconstitutional.

Rabbi Daniel Lapin, an Orthodox Jewish leader, is the founder and director of Toward Tradition:

Who are those leading the charge, those who are most aggressive, most ferocious, and most determined to extirpate any lingering remnant of biblical civilization of Judeo-Christian culture from America?... In attempting to analyze the *Storm Troopers of Secularism,* I put the American Civil Liberties Union, the ACLU, very high up on that list....

It is not an accident that America has provided the most tranquil haven of prosperity that Jews have enjoyed in 2,000 years, and that's because America is a Christian nation—it's not in spite of that. I think always of America's Bible Belt as Judaism's safety belt. And the reality here is that in countries that have stripped away Christian foundations, what's left is not nothing, but the intrusion of values that are hostile to all forms of faith.[11]

But the ACLU has deceived many people concerning their real agenda. Alan Sears noted:

The ACLU is a master at public relations. They postured, they positioned themselves wonderfully through the years, with their media, with their advertising, with their public relations efforts, and most Americans think that the ACLU is a disinterested, third-party sort of a monitor on the government, who'll sort of set out and watch and monitor and make sure that our civil rights are not impended. When in truth, in fact, the ACLU has a very clear agenda…is very driven to advance its own goals, its own philosophy.… If the ACLU had its way, we would have a religion-free America. All of the basic tenets of Christianity and orthodox Judaism would disappear from the public square.…

I actually call the ACLU the number-one religious censor in America because basically, for five to six decades, they've been using the courts, they've been bringing action after action, looking for activist judges, looking for courts that would basically reinterpret and redefine what the Founders meant and limit the rights of the public and the people of faith.[12]

The ACLU has done incredible damage to the interpretation of the Constitution and to our understanding of what the Founding Fathers intended. The ACLU is on record as opposing virtually every positive aspect of Christian faith and morality, and it is on record as favoring virtually every perversion imaginable, even the distribution of child pornography.[13]

ACLU official Burt Neuborne made an astounding statement: "I would not want to live in a world where the ACLU won all its cases."[14]

Would you?

I believe Jesus would have us be wary of such an organization.

A GODLY FOUNDATION

The history books are being rewritten, and God is being systematically erased. The Judeo-Christian tradition built this nation in a unique way, and a nation that forgets its past has no future. But in the name of "separation of church and state," terrible things are happening across the country nearly every day. Take the recent example of a professor who might get fired at a California junior college—even though he is tenured. Why the censure? Around Thanksgiving in 2006, he dared to send an e-mail to fellow professors that contained George Washington's Thanksgiving Proclamation, which, of course, mentions God. Washington began that Congressionally endorsed proclamation: "It is the duty of all nations to acknowledge the Providence of Almighty God, to obey His will, to be grateful for his benefits, and humbly to implore His protection and favor."[15]

Consider the case involving an atheist who sued to remove the words "under God" from the Pledge of Allegiance. He is the same man who has tried to get rid of some other things in our country that mention God. He makes it a private crusade to scratch out "under God" on all the currency that goes through his hands. His lawsuits against the pledge have caused some schools to stop saying it until the courts sort through the issues.

In 1955 Dwight D. Eisenhower said, "Without God, there could be no American form of Government, nor an American way of life. Recognition of the Supreme Being is the first—the most basic—expression of Americanism. Thus the founding fathers of America saw it, and thus with God's help, it will continue to be."[16] Yet atheists today gnash their teeth when they hear anyone publicly acknowledge God.

So I ask, Who is out of step with our history?

Secularists want us to believe that this nation is not a nation under God. I have heard people say numerous times that this was never a Christian nation and was never founded as such. Go back to 1606. The landing at Plymouth Rock was yet fourteen years away. In that year those who left England and founded Jamestown in 1607 did so for a very specific reason. In 1606, before they left England, they drew up the first charter of Virginia, which states, "We are greatly commending, and graciously accepting of, their desires for the furtherance of so noble a work, which may, by the providence of Almighty God, hereafter tend to the glory of His Divine Majesty, in propagating of Christian religion to such people as yet live in darkness and miserable ignorance of the true knowledge and worship of God."[17] But in 2007, at the official celebration of Jamestown's four hundredth anniversary, the name of Jesus Christ was prohibited.

In 1620, when the Pilgrims landed in America, they gathered in the captain's cabin just before going ashore and wrote the birth certificate of America: the Mayflower Compact. Many people see this as the beginning of America. The compact begins with these words: "In the Name of God, Amen.... Having undertaken for the glory of God, and advancement of the Christian Faith, and the Honour of our King and Country, a Voyage to plant the first Colony in the Northern parts of Virginia."[18]

According to the man who recorded much of the history of that colony, William Bradford, the first thing the Pilgrims did upon landing was "they fell upon their knees and blessed the God of Heaven."[19] And in Jamestown the first act performed by the settlers was the erection of a large wooden cross on governmentally chartered land.

America's first complete constitution, the Fundamental Orders of Connecticut, written in 1639, states: "Forasmuch as it hath pleased the Almighty God by the wise disposition of his divine providence so to order and dispose of things that we...enter into combination and confederation together to maintain and preserve the liberty and purity of the gospel of our Lord Jesus."[20]

In 1643 (twenty years after the Pilgrims landed), for the first time, all of the settlements that became the various communities of the Northeast joined to form the New England Confederation. There, they declared:

"Whereas we all came into these parts of America with one and the same end and aim, namely, to advance the kingdom of our Lord Jesus Christ and to enjoy the liberties of the Gospel in purity with peace."[21]

The Declaration of Independence states, "We hold these truths to be self-evident, that all men are created equal, that they are endowed by their Creator with certain unalienable rights, that among these are life, liberty, and the pursuit of happiness."[22]

Be certain of this: if our rights and liberties do not come from God, they are not inalienable. The state gives and the state takes away, according to its own pleasure. If the state is in charge of endowing our rights and liberties, then they are very alienable and subject to the whims of totalitarian rule. Without God, the state becomes the final authority, and that is totalitarianism, possibly despotism. As a matter of fact, that is exactly what the French established in France shortly after the American Revolution—all rights of all people were bestowed by the state. And from the history books about the French Revolution, we know that shortly after the founding of that republic, blood flowed in the streets of Paris.

Recently our local paper, the *South Florida Sun-Sentinel*, reported that someone said he did not want to acknowledge America as a nation under God because he wanted the people to be sovereign. Fortunately, no such possibility exists. That is the lie. The reality is that when people establish themselves as sovereign, you soon find yourself living in a sovereign state that is telling you what to do. That is what happened in Nazi Germany. That is what happened in the Soviet Union. The great promise of social justice for all was trumpeted from the stages, promoting the rights of the proletariat, the rights of the people. And ultimately, in such situations, the people end up with no rights at all. Whether you call it humanism, secularism, Marxism, socialism, or "power to the people," it is a fundamental flaw in the human system that causes such innocent notions to allow governments to amass power and use it to control people despotically.

Most of the Founders of this nation were Christians, with very few exceptions—about 5 percent. In fact, it is hard to find more than 5 of the 250 people considered to be Founding Fathers who are not easily identified as Christians. George Washington was a devout Christian. Modern secularists have attempted to rip him out of his eighteenth-century Anglican context, but they have failed. You can read the evidence of Washington for yourself in the carefully researched and detailed work *George Washington's Sacred Fire* by Peter Lillback with Jerry Newcombe.[23] Washington served as a leader in a church that proclaimed, "We are accounted righteous before God only for the merit of our Lord and Saviour Jesus Christ, by faith, and not for our own works or deservings."[24] Washington wrote to the Delaware tribe chiefs: "You do well to wish to learn our arts and ways of life, and above all, the religion of Jesus Christ. These will make you a greater and happier people than you are."[25]

When Washington was inaugurated as the first president, he placed his hand upon a Bible. When he took the oath of office, he kissed the Bible and then led the whole Congress to St. Paul's Chapel for a two-hour service of worship and thanksgiving. Very shortly after his inauguration, a group of people asked him to declare a national day of thanksgiving. Obviously, these people were ignorant of the true "separation of church and state." They would have known that no such thing was permitted by the Constitution. Yet those people were the Congress who had just written and passed the Constitution.[26]

Again, Washington's Thanksgiving proclamation states, "Whereas it is the duty of all nations to acknowledge the providence of Almighty God, to obey His will, to be grateful for His benefits, and humbly implore His protection and favor."[27] He goes on to call the nation to thankfulness to Almighty God. "It is the duty of all nations," said the father of our country, "to obey His will," which Washington believed could be found in the Ten Commandments.[28] And yet, for repeating this proclamation, an Arizona professor might lose his job.

I have made it a point to read the inaugural addresses of all our presidents. I discovered something that I think might interest you. In every address, without exception, the presidents mention almighty God—either by referring to Him as such or imploring His aid. Furthermore, each state constitution contains, without exception, an appeal or a prayer to almighty God:

★ "We, the people of the State of North Carolina, grateful to Almighty God, the Sovereign ruler of nations, for the preservation of the American Union and the existence of our civil, political, and religious liberties."[29]

★ [The Vermont Constitution:] "That all men have a natural and unalienable right, to worship Almighty God, according to the dictates of their own consciences."[30]

★ "We, the People of the State of New York, grateful to Almighty God for our Freedom, in order to secure its blessings, do establish this Constitution."[31]

The monuments of our country also bear indelible testimony to our national faith in God. The cornerstone of the Capitol was laid by George Washington himself. Later a metal box was inserted that contained documents believed worthy of preservation and remembrance. The dedication at that ceremony was given by the great statesman Daniel Webster, who said, "And all here assembled, whether belonging to public life or to private life, with hearts devoutly thankful to Almighty God for the preservation of the liberty and happiness of the country, unite in sincere and fervent prayer, that this deposit, and the walls and arches, the domes and towers, the columns and the entablatures, now to be erected over it may endure forever. God save the United States of America."[32]

If you were to go inside the Capitol, you would find scores of sculptures and paintings that mostly have to do with the great Christians and events that took place in the founding of this country. Go to the House of Representatives or the Senate. Carved in the wall is the national motto, "In God we trust." At the Supreme Court building, a carving on the entablature depicts Moses holding the two tablets of the Law. One state attorney general pointed out that there are twenty different representations of Moses and the Ten Commandments in the building. (There are those who say that the Ten Commandments should not be found in our courtrooms.)

If you were to wait until the justices enter the courtroom, you would hear the crier announce, "Oyez! Oyez! Oyez! All persons having business before the Honorable, the Supreme Court of the United States, are admonished to draw near and give their attention, for the Court is now sitting. God save the United States and this Honorable Court!"[33]

At the White House, the first inhabitant, John Adams, had carved over the fireplace in one of the large dining rooms: "I pray Heaven to bestow the best of Blessings on this House and all that shall hereafter inhabit it."[34]

The Washington Monument, which is dedicated to our first president and the father of our country, contains numerous Scripture references or Scripture-oriented phrases:

- ★ "God and our native land."
- ★ "Search the Scriptures." (John 5:39, KJV)

★ "Holiness unto the LORD." (Zechariah 14:20, KJV)

★ "Suffer the little children to come unto me, and forbid them not: for of such is the kingdom of God." (Mark 10:14, KJV)

★ "Train up a child in the way he should go: and when he is old, he will not depart from it." (Proverbs 22:6, KJV)

★ "In God we trust."

★ "May heaven to this union continue its beneficence."[35]

If you were to reach the great pinnacle of that monument, there in the metal cap at the top, on the outside, you would see beautifully engraved the words: "Praise be to God"[36] (in Latin). That monument towers over the entire city of Washington, D.C.

The rooms of the Library of Congress contain much the same:

★ "The heavens declare the glory of God; and the firmament sheweth His handywork." (Psalm 19:1, KJV)[37]

★ "Wisdom is the principal thing; therefore get wisdom: and with all thy getting get understanding." (Proverbs 4:7, KJV)[38]

★ "What doth the LORD require of thee, but to do justly, and to love mercy, and to walk humbly with thy God?" (Micah 6:8, KJV)[39]

★ "One God, one element, and one far-off divine event to which the whole creation moves." (Alfred Tennyson)[40]

★ "Nature is the art of God." (Thomas Brown)[41]

On the walls of the monuments clustered around the National Mall, Lincoln's Memorial contains the Gettysburg Address: "That this nation, under God, shall have a new birth of freedom; and that government of the people, by the people, for the people shall not perish from the earth."[42] The Jefferson Memorial contains the words: "Almighty God hath created the mind free."[43]

Francis Scott Key included the phrase "Praise the Pow'r that hath made and preserved us a nation!… And this be our motto, 'In God is our trust!" in "The Star-Spangled Banner," our national anthem.[44]

Historically, our nation honored God, His Word, and His Son.

In 1892 the Supreme Court issued the famed Trinity decision. The justices spent *ten years* studying every document having anything to do with the foundation of America. In a unanimous ruling, they declared, "We find everywhere a clear definition of the same truth…this is a Christian nation."[45]

TIME TO ACT

A few years ago, before the 2006 election, Congress acted on the issue of whether or not this nation is "under God." Nearly unanimously, the House of Representatives voted to reaffirm the words "one nation under God" in the Pledge of Allegiance and also to reaffirm our national motto, "In God we trust." In the Senate, the vote was unanimous.

When a California judge ruled on getting rid of "under God," it was on the front page of every newspaper in the country. But when "under God" was reaffirmed, somehow our local newspaper did not find that newsworthy.

I believe something can be done. I know a man who shared those feelings. He said, "There is simply no historical foundation for the proposition that the Framers intended to build 'the wall of separation'…'between church and State.' [It] is a metaphor based on bad history, a metaphor which has proved useless as a guide to judging. It should be frankly and explicitly abandoned."[46]

Who said that? William Rehnquist, the late chief justice of the Supreme Court. There is no such "wall of separation" in the Constitution. There is nothing in the first ten amendments to it. There is nothing in the

First Amendment about it. No mention of church, state, or separation. It is not in any of our founding documents—nor was it intended to be.

You'll remember that I said before, I am not calling for a theocracy in America. However, the Founding Fathers did not give us a government they expected us to change. Someone asked me if I was out to Christianize America. I responded, "No, of course not. I'm out to Christianize the whole world." What else does the Great Commission mean but that? We are to proclaim the gospel to all people and pray that they will respond positively to the invitation to receive Christ and the gift of eternal life. If they do, they will become Christians, and that will result in a greater "Christianization" of any country where they live.

It's amazing that is seen as somehow un-American or alien or foreign, whereas 99.8 percent of the people in this country as late as 1776 professed themselves to be Christians.[47] The idea that we would Christianize this country is only an effort to return the country to its roots. Anything less would be to introduce something foreign, alien, unplanned. Seventy-eight percent of those living in America still profess themselves to be Christians.[48] We have a higher percentage of Christians in this country than anywhere else on earth. Even outspoken atheist and writer Sam Harris admits that we live in a Christian nation in his book *Letter to a Christian Nation*. And although he hopes to talk us out of being one, there is no doubt about where we began.

It's time we got back to those historical roots and took back our heritage as a nation unified under one almighty God. I believe Jesus would have us vote in a way that would increase religious liberty.

Notes

Foreword

1. Anna Quindlen, "Disinvited to the Party: Why Giuliani's Candidacy Could Be a Good Thing for the GOP," *Newsweek*, September 3, 2007.

Chapter 1: Do Jesus and Politics Mix?

1. James Dobson, quoted in Bob Unruh, "'They Just Don't Get It' Is Why Republicans Lost," WorldNetDaily.com, November 9, 2006, www.world netdaily.com/news/article.asp?ARTICLE_ID=52884.
2. Unruh, "'They Just Don't Get It' Is Why Republicans Lost."
3. "GOP Dips in Religion Poll," AP, *NewsMax*, November 2006, 11, www.newsmax.com/archives/ic/2006/8/24/193421.shtml?s=tn.
4. Jon Meacham, "The Politics of Jesus," *Newsweek*, November 13, 2006.
5. Jim Wallis, "The Religious Right's Era Is Over," *Time*, February 16, 2007.
6. Christian Newswire, February 19, 2007, www.christiannewswire.com/news/924012282.html.
7. Hillary Clinton, C-Span, June 21, 2004, quoted in *NewsMax*, January 2007, 60.
8. Hillary Hires Evangelical Consultant," *NewsMax*, December 26, 2006, www.newsmax.com/archives/ic/2006/12/26/122609.shtml?s=al &promo_code=2B60–1.
9. Don Feder, "To Fight 'Fascism,' New York Times' Author Wants to Ban Religious Right," GrassTopsUSA Exclusive Commentary, January 16, 2007.
10. William L. Shirer, *The Rise and Fall of the Third Reich* (New York: Simon and Schuster, 1960), 237.
11. Abraham Lincoln, quoted in J. B. McClure, ed., *Abraham Lincoln's Stories and Speeches* (Chicago: Rhodes & McClure, 1896), 185–86.

12. Of the twenty-seven books in the New Testament canon, the only one in which the author is unknown is Hebrews. However, there was a very early tradition that Paul wrote Hebrews, and that is why it was accepted as holy writ. Eusebius wrote in the fourth century: "The epistle to the Hebrews [Clement of Alexandria] attributes to Paul but says that it was written in Hebrew for Hebrews and then carefully translated by Luke for the Greeks. Therefore the translation has the same style and color as Acts. [The prefatory] 'Paul, an apostle' was naturally omitted, as Clement says: 'In writing to Hebrews prejudiced against him and suspicious of him, he wisely did not offend them at the start by adding his name'" (Paul L. Maier, ed., *Eusebius: The Church History* [Grand Rapids: Kregel, 1996], 217–18). Whoever the author of Hebrews was, we believe the book to have been divinely written and divinely chosen to be in the canon, just like the other twenty-six books of the New Testament and the thirty-nine books of the Old Testament.

13. Dan Brown, *The Da Vinci Code* (New York: Doubleday, 2003), 248.

14. George Barna, *Absolute Confusion: How Our Moral and Spiritual Foundations Are Eroding in This Age of Change* (Ventura, CA: Regal, 1993), 86–87.

15. See www.bpnews.net/printerfriendly.asp?ID=24385.

16. Martin Luther King Jr., *The Wisdom of Martin Luther King in His Own Words* (New York: Lancer, 1968), 106.

17. C. S. Lewis, *Mere Christianity* (New York: Macmillan, 1960), 51.

18. Such changes are the subject of two of our earlier books: *What If Jesus Had Never Been Born?* (Nashville: Thomas Nelson, 1994) and *What If the Bible Had Never Been Written?* (Nashville: Thomas Nelson, 1998).

19. Lorraine Boettner, *The Millennium* (Phillipsburg, NJ: Presbyterian and Reformed Publishing, 1957), 33.

20. For those who know what the term means, I am not a *theonomist*—one who feels the civil laws of the Old Testament apply today. Nor do I advocate stoning homosexuals. Ninety-nine percent of Christians in this country are not of that school of thought, and I certainly am not. I would indeed oppose it if it were ever seriously considered.

21. Robert T. Michael et al., *Sex in America: A Definitive Survey* (Boston: Little, Brown, 1994), 176.

22. George Gallup Jr., interview by Jerry Newcombe, Coral Ridge Ministries-TV, August 1999.

23. University of Akron Survey Research Center, *National Survey of Religion and Politics 1992,* cited in *Time,* January 30, 1995, 75.

24. C. S. Lewis, *Mere Christianity,* quoted in Wayne Martindale and Jerry Root, eds., *The Quotable Lewis* (Wheaton, IL: Tyndale, 1989), 305–6.

25. John Calvin, quoted by R. C. Sproul, *Renewing Your Mind,* radio program, April 24, 2001.

Chapter 2: Render unto Caesar

1. Rees Lloyd, interview by Christina Vidal, Coral Ridge Ministries-TV, June 2005.

2. Bill Federer, interview by Jerry Newcombe, Coral Ridge Ministries-TV, December 2004.

3. *Crockett v. Sorenson,* 568 F.Supp. 1422, 1425–1430 (W.D. Va. 1983), quoted in William J. Federer, *American Quotations* (St. Louis, MO: Amerisearch Inc., 2002), CD-ROM.

4. "First Settlement of New England: A Discourse Delivered at Plymouth, on the 22nd of December, 1820," in *The Great Speeches and Orations of Daniel Webster with an Essay on Daniel Webster as a Master of English Style, by Edwin P. Whipple* (Boston, Little Brown and Company, 1879), 51.

5. Samuel Adams, "The Rights of the Colonists as Christians," in *The Annals of America,* vol. 2, *1755–1783: Resistance and Revolution* (Chicago: Encyclopaedia Britannica, 1976), 219.

6. George Washington, to the Synod of Dutch Reformed Church in North America, October 9, 1789, in Paul F. Boller Jr., *George Washington and Religion* (Dallas: Southern Methodist University Press, 1963), 178.

7. John Quincy Adams, quoted in J. Wingate Thornton, *The Pulpit of the American Revolution* (Boston: Gould & Lincoln, 1860), quoted in Verna M. Hall, comp., *The Christian History of the Constitution of the United States of America* (San Francisco: Foundation for American Christian Education, 1960), 372.

8. George Washington, "Farewell Address," in John Rhodehamel, comp., *George Washington: Writings* (New York: Literary Classics of the United States, 1997), 971.

9. Daniel Webster, *The Works of Daniel Webster*, 6 vols. (Boston: Little, Brown, 1853), 1:22, quoted in Gary DeMar, *God and Government: A Biblical and Historical Study* (Atlanta: American Vision Press, 1984), xiii.

10. Joseph Story, *Commentaries on the Constitution of the United States*, 2nd ed., vol. 2 (Boston: Charles C. Little and James Brown, 1851), 593–94, quoted in Robert L. Cord, *Separation of Church and State: Historical Fact and Current Fiction* (Grand Rapids: Baker, 1988), 13.

11. Charles Hodge, *Systematic Theology*, 3 vols. (Grand Rapids: Eerdmans, 1970), 3:345–46.

12. "First Charter of Virginia," in *The Annals of America*, vol. 1, *1493–1754: Discovering a New World* (Chicago: Encyclopaedia Britannica, 1976), 16.

13. John Jay, *The Correspondence and Public Papers of John Jay*, Henry P. Johnston, ed. (NY: Burt Franklin, 1970), 4:393, quoted in William J. Federer, *America's God and Country Encyclopedia of Quotations* (St. Louis: AmeriSearch, 2000), 318.

Chapter 3: Salt and Light

1. Donald E. Wildmon, "300,000 Silent Pulpits," *CBA Bulletin*, vol. 3, no. 12, Citizen's Bar Association.

2. H. Henry Meeter, *The Basic Idea of Calvinism* (Grand Rapids: Kregel, 1956), 91, www.jackfritscher.com/PDF/TennWilliams/love&dth.pdf.

3. W. S. Reid, quoted in J. D. Douglas, gen. ed., *The New International Dictionary of the Christian Church* (Grand Rapids: Zondervan, 1978), 179.

Chapter 4: Matters of Life and Death

1. Michael Behe, interview by Jerry Newcombe, WAFG radio, Ft. Lauderdale, FL, July 2, 1998.

2. Malcolm Muggeridge, quoted in Ronald Reagan, *Abortion and the Conscience of the Nation* (Nashville: Thomas Nelson, 1984), 83.

3. Steven Ertelt, "Pro-Life Advocates Won Majority of Races Against Abortion Advocates," LifeNews.com, November 10, 2006.

4. Ertelt, "Pro-Life Advocates Won."

5. Quoted in Ertelt, "Pro-Life Advocates Won."

6. See "Report of the South Dakota Task Force to Study Abortion," December 2005, www.voteyesforlife.com/docs/Task_Force_Report.pdf.

7. Allen Unruh and Leslee Unruh, Reclaiming America for Christ Conference, Coral Ridge Ministries, Fort Lauderdale, FL, 2006.

8. Unruh and Unruh, Reclaiming America for Christ Conference.

9. "Report of the South Dakota Task Force to Study Abortion," www.voteyesforlife.com/docs/Task_Force_Report.pdf.

10. Right to Life of Michigan, "A View of Human Embryo Stem Cell Research," 2, www.rtl.org/html/pdf/Stem_Cell_Research_follow_the_money.pdf.

11. Michael Fumento, "Code of Silence," Daily Standard, February 8, 2007, www.fumento.com/biotech/stemce112007.html.

12. Dr. David Prentice, senior fellow for life sciences for Family Research Council in Washington, DC, points out that part of the reason embryonic-stem-cell research has been unsuccessful so far (and will likely be unsuccessful in the future) is because the job description of an embryonic stem cell is to grow as fast as possible and to start making every tissue at once. The Journal of Neurology reports that during the 1990s, researchers attempted to heal patients with Parkinson's by using the tissue of aborted unborn babies (with cells similar to embryonic stem cells). None of the patients was cured. In many, the cells grew too well and overproduced needed brain chemicals. In one case the embryonic-stem-cell tissue caused teeth and hair to grow in the patient's brain, killing the patient. Remember: the job of an embryonic stem cell is to grow fast and make everything at once. Meanwhile, all the successful treatments involving stem cells (73 so far) have been with adult stem cells, which pro-lifers embrace. So why the constant push for embryonic-stem-cell-research funding? (Telephone conversation with Jerry Newcombe, June 22, 2007. For more information, see www.stemcellresearch.org.)

13. For example, here is what Surgeon General C. Everett Koop wrote about the pre-Holocaust killing and the slippery slope:

Medical science in Nazi Germany collaborated with this Hegelian trend, particularly in the following enterprises: the mass extermination of the chronically sick in the interest of saving "useless" expenses to the community as a whole; the mass extermination of those considered socially disturbing or racially and ideologically unwanted; the individual, the inconspicuous extermination of those considered disloyal to the ruling group; and the ruthless use of human experimental material in medical military research. Remember, physicians took part in this planning.

Adults were propagandized; one outstanding example being a motion picture called *I Accuse,* which dealt with euthanasia. This film depicted the life history of a woman suffering from multiple sclerosis and eventually showed her husband, a doctor, killing her to accompaniment of soft piano music played by a sympathetic colleague in an adjacent room. The ideology was implanted even in high school children when their mathematics texts included problems stated in distorted terms of the cost of caring for and rehabilitating the chronically sick and crippled. For example, one problem asked how many new housing units could be built and how many marriage-allowance loans could be given to newlyweds for the amount of money it cost the state to care for "the crippled, the criminal, and the insane." This was all before Hitler. And it was all in the hands of the medical profession.

The first direct order for euthanasia came from Hitler in 1939. All state institutions were required to report on patients who had been ill for five years or more or who were unable to work. (C. Everett Koop, quoted in Ronald Reagan, *Abortion and the Conscience of the Nation* [Nashville: Thomas Nelson Publishers, 1984], 61–63)

14. Charles Krauthammer, "The Netherlands Experience," *Human Events,* November 9, 1991.

15. Charles Hodge, *Systematic Theology,* 3 vols. (Grand Rapids: Eerdmans, 1952), 3:367.

16. George W. Bush, "National Sanctity of Human Life Day, 2003: A Proclamation," The White House, www.whitehouse.gov/news/releases/2003/01/20030114-13.html.

Chapter 5: Crime and Punishment

1. Hebden Taylor, *The New Legality: In the Light of the Christian Philosophy of Law* (Philadelphia: Presbyterian and Reformed Publishing, 1967), v.
2. Taylor, *New Legality*, vi.
3. C. S. Lewis, "The Humanitarian Theory of Punishment," *Essays on the Death Penalty* (Houston: St. Thomas Press, n.d.), 3, quoted in Taylor, *New Legality*, 24–25.
4. Carl F. H. Henry, *Christian Personal Ethics* (Grand Rapids: Eerdmans, 1957), 305.
5. M. Stanton Evans, "Statistics Show Case for Capital Punishment," *Human Events*, May 3, 1975.
6. U.S. Constitution, amend. 8, quoted in *The World Almanac and Book of Facts 2003* (New York: World Almanac Books, 2003), 548.
7. U.S. Constitution, amend. 5, quoted in *World Almanac and Book of Facts 2003*, 548.
8. Dennis Prager, "Another Argument for Capital Punishment," WorldNetDaily.com, December 12, 2006, www.wnd.com/news/article.asp?article_id=53331.
9. Prager, "Another Argument for Capital Punishment."
10. Prager writes: "In 1982, James Ealy was convicted of the strangulation murders of a family—including a mother and her two children. It took the jury just four hours to render the guilty verdict, and Ealy was sentenced to life in prison without the possibility of parole. However, his lawyers argued that the police had improperly obtained evidence, and an Illinois appellate court, whose justices acknowledged Ealy was guilty of the murders, vacated the ruling. But without that improperly obtained evidence, Ealy could not be retried successfully, and he was released from prison.

    "On Nov. 27, 2006, Ealy strangled to death Mary Hutchison, a 45-year-old manager of a Burger King in Lindenhurst, Ill.

    "That woman was killed because many Americans believe that it is better to let a murderer go free than to convict one with evidence improperly obtained.

    "Whether that position is right or wrong is not relevant here. What is relevant is this: The people who believe in this policy do so knowing that it will lead to the murder of innocent people like Mary Hutchison, just as I believe in capital punishment knowing that it might lead to the killing of an innocent person. So those who still wish to argue for keeping all murderers alive will need to argue something other than 'an innocent may be killed.' They already support a policy that ensures innocents will be killed."

Chapter 6: War: Is It Ever Justified?

1. Samuel Pearce, *Motives to Gratitude* (Birmingham, AL: Belcher, 1798), 18–19.
2. Gleason Archer, *The Encyclopedia of Bible Difficulties* (Grand Rapids: Zondervan, 1982), 219.
3. Robert A. Morey, *When Is It Right to Fight?* (Minneapolis: Bethany, 1978), 34.
4. Leslie Carbone, "The Cost of Abandoning 'Great Things,'" Breakpoint, January 25, 2007, www.breakpoint.org/listingarticle.asp?ID=6024.
5. Patrick Henry, "Give Me Liberty or Give Me Death," March 23, 1775, in *The Annals of America*, vol. 2, *1755–1783: Resistance and Revolution* (Chicago: Encyclopaedia Britannica, 1976), 323.
6. George Bancroft, *History of the United States of America, from the Discovery of the Continent,* 6 vols. (New York: Appleton, 1859), 1:178.
7. Bancroft, *History of the United States of America,* 1:178.
8. Quoted in Os Guinness, *The Great Experiment* (Colorado Springs: NavPress, 2001), 64.
9. Even in Northern Ireland, the conflicts are political (British versus Irish), not religious (Catholic versus Protestant). However, I will concede that religion adds fuel to the fire. Thankfully, that violence has tapered off in recent years.
10. Bill O'Reilly, "Pray for Peace but Polish the Weapons," *Washington Times,* April 22–28, 2002, 35.

Chapter 7: Education and Our Schools

1. Cited in John Eidsmoe, *Christianity and the Constitution: The Faith of Our Founding Fathers* (Grand Rapids: Baker, 1987), 22.
2. Benjamin R. Barber, *Sunshine,* March 13, 1994.

3. Quoted in Dennis L. Cuddy, "A Chronology of Education with Quotable Quotes," *Florida Forum,* May 1993, 3–4.

4. Thomas Sowell, *Inside American Education: The Decline, the Deception, the Dogmas* (New York: Free Press, 1993), 3.

5. *Tropic,* a publication of the *Miami Herald,* September 27, 1987.

6. Phyllis Schlafly, "What's Going On in Public Schools?" *Rutherford,* September 1992, 11.

7. Mary Jordan, "U.S. Falling Behind in Teaching the Basics," *Washington Post,* May 5, 1994.

8. Paul Blanshard, "Three Cheers for Our Secular State," *The Humanist* 17 (April 1976), www.christianparents.com/outline.htm.

9. George Washington, "Farewell Address," September 19, 1796, in *The Annals of America,* vol. 3, *1784–1796: Organizing the New Nation* (Chicago: Encyclopaedia Britannica, 1976), 612.

10. Northwest Ordinance, Article III, in *The Annals of America,* vol. 3, *1784–1796: Organizing the New Nation* (Chicago: Encyclopaedia Britannica, 1976), 194–95.

11. William Holmes McGuffey, *McGuffey's Sixth Eclectic Reader,* EBook #16751, www.gutenberg.org/etext/16751.

12. See Samuel L. Blumenfeld, "Enter Horace Mann," chap. 9 in *Is Public Education Necessary?* (Boise, ID: Paradigm Company, 1985).

13. Barbara Walters, quoted in Charles Colson with Nancy R. Pearcey, *A Dangerous Grace: Daily Readings* (Dallas: Word, 1994), 266.

14. Deistic, atheistic Founding Fathers represented a small portion of the total picture. David Barton, author of *Original Intent,* points out that approximately 250 men could be called our Founding Fathers. They served on the Continental Congresses; they gave us the Declaration of Independence, the Articles of Confederation, the Constitution, the Bill of Rights, the Northwest Ordinance. Of these 250 men, about a dozen, less than 5 percent, were not orthodox Christians. These include Thomas Jefferson, Benjamin Franklin, Thomas Paine, and Ethan Allen. But even these men were pro-Bible and had something of a Christian worldview.

(Paine later completely rejected such a worldview, but when he wrote *Common Sense* in 1776, he referred positively to the Bible.) Jefferson and Franklin were not anti-Christian skeptics, as they are portrayed today. Modern secularists often quote this handful of men as if they represent the total picture. This is misleading and dishonest. The exception proves the rule, but the exception is not the rule. This is a shell game of the worst kind, but unfortunately millions of Americans today are exposed to this type of shell game, and they never hear the other side.

15. "Is Declaration of Independence Unconstitutional? School District Sued for Censoring Founding Documents, State Constitutions," WorldNetDaily, November 23, 2004, www.worldnetdaily.com/news/article.asp ?ARTICLE_ID=41623.

16. A. A. Hodge, *Popular Lectures on Theological Themes* (Philadelphia: Presbyterian Board of Publications, 1887), 283.

17. Paul Kurtz, *Humanist Manifestos I and II* (Buffalo, NY: Prometheus Books, 1981), 15.

18. Kurtz, *Humanist Manifestos I and II,* 15.

19. Jacques Barzun, quoted in Joseph Adelson, *Inventing Adolescence: The Political Psychology of Everyday Schooling* (New Brunswick, NJ: Transaction Books, 1986), 16.

Chapter 8: Economic Concerns

1. Richard Land, interview by Jerry Newcombe, *Vocal Point,* WAFG Radio, Fort Lauderdale, April 13, 2007.

2. See Rousas Rushdoony, *Politics of Guilt and Pity* (Nutley, NJ: Craig Press, 1970).

3. No one knows for sure the exact source of this prediction. A search through the writings of Alexis de Tocqueville, one of those to whom these words are commonly attributed, yields no results. Sometimes this quote is attributed to Alexander Tytler, who later became Lord Alexander Fraser Woodhouselee. The source of the quote may be Tytler's *Universal History* or his *Elements of General History, Ancient and Modern,* as they contain extensive discussions of the political systems in historic civilizations, including Athens. *Universal*

History was published after, and based upon, *Elements of General History,* which was a collection of Professor Tytler's lecture notes.

4. Rus Walton, *One Nation Under God* (Nashville: Thomas Nelson, 1987), 96.

5. Thomas Sowell, quoted in John Jefferson Davis, *Your Wealth in God's World: Does the Bible Support the Free Market?* (Phillipsburg, NJ: Presbyterian and Reformed Publishing, 1984), 59.

6. Larry Burkett, *The Coming Economic Earthquake* (Chicago: Moody, 1991), 226.

7. Leland Ryken, *Worldly Saints: The Puritans as They Really Were* (Grand Rapids: Zondervan, 1990), 238.

8. Georgia Harkness, *John Calvin: The Man and His Ethics* (New York: Henry Holt, 1931), 54.

9. The year of this particular statistic, which comes from the Food and Nutrition Service, U.S. Department of Agriculture, is 1999. See *The World Almanac and Book of Facts 2001* (Mahwah, NJ: World Almanac Books, 2001), 155.

10. These statistics apply to fiscal year 2000 from the Financial Management Service, U.S. Department of the Treasury, cited in *World Almanac and Book of Facts 2001,* 127–28.

11. Frank Wright, former director of the D. James Kennedy Center for Christian Statesmanship and current director of the National Religious Broadcasters (NRB), earned his PhD in economics. He points out that not all of what we could call "social spending" are transfer payments. He wrote, "A workable definition of transfer payments would be: money given by the government to its citizens. Examples would include Social Security, unemployment compensation, welfare, and disability payments. The determining factor would seem to be direct payments made to individuals. Broad-based public health expenditures, trust fund payments, and administrative expenses might be examples of the true costs of a welfare state, but they would likely not be counted as transfer payments" (e-mail to Jerry Newcombe, January 3, 2003).

12. Cheryl Wetzstein, "Welfare Study Shows Ideas Changing," *Washington Times,* November 25–December 1, 2002, 14.

13. Mark Trumbull, "As US Tax Rates Drop, Government's Reach Grows," *Christian Science Monitor,* April 16, 2007, www.csmonitor.com/ 2007/0416/p01s04-usec.html.

Chapter 9: Health-Care Issues

1. Bill Clinton, Southern Legislature Conference (Miami, FL, August 11, 1992).
2. Christopher Ruddy, "Healthcare Dilemma," *NewsMax,* June 2007, 90.
3. Ed Haislmaier, interview by Jerry Newcombe, Coral Ridge Ministries-TV, December 2, 1993.
4. Burke Balch, interview by Jerry Newcombe, Coral Ridge Ministries-TV, December 2, 1993.
5. Chris Smith (R-NJ), interview by Jerry Newcombe, Coral Ridge Ministries-TV, December 2, 1993.
6. Balch, interview by Jerry Newcombe.
7. Cal Thomas, interview by Jerry Newcombe, Coral Ridge Ministries-TV, December 3, 1993.
8. Smith, interview by Jerry Newcombe.
9. Richard Fenigsen, interview by John Adams, Coral Ridge Ministries-TV, December 15, 1993.
10. Paul Maier in D. James Kennedy, *What If Jesus Had Never Been Born?* video (Ft. Lauderdale: Coral Ridge Ministries-TV, 2006).
11. Remarks of Dutch man in D. James Kennedy, *Who Lives? Who Dies? Who Cares?* video (Ft. Lauderdale, FL: Coral Ridge Ministries-TV, 1994).
12. Balch, interview by Jerry Newcombe.
13. Haislmaier, interview by Jerry Newcombe.
14. *Steve Kane Show,* May 28, 2007.
15. Ruddy, "Healthcare Dilemma," 90.
16. Mark Steyn, "Pies in the Sky," *New York Sun,* June 18, 2007, http://www.nysun.com/article/56792?page_no=2.
17. Balch, interview by Jerry Newcombe.
18. Bev Larson and Randy Larson, interview by Jerry Newcombe, Coral Ridge Ministries-TV, December 16, 1993.
19. Ruddy, "Healthcare Dilemma," 90.

Chapter 10: The Environment and Climate Change

1. Peter Gwynne, "The Cooling World," *Newsweek*, April 28, 1975, www.rushlimbaugh.com/home/eibessentia12/april_28__1975 _newsweek___the_cooling_world___by_peter_gwynne.guest.html.

2. S. Fred Singer and Dennis T. Avery, *Unstoppable Global Warming Every 1,500 Years* (Lanham, MD: Rowman & Littlefield, 2007).

3. Laurie Goodstein, "86 Evangelical Leaders Join to Fight Global Warming," *New York Times*, February 8, 2006.

4. At the time we signed the document in 2006, it was titled Interfaith Stewardship Alliance.

5. "Evangelical Leaders Exploited by Global Warming—Population Control Lobby," Christian Newswire, September 29, 2006, www.acton.org/ article.php?article=205.

6. "Nuremberg-Style Trials Proposed for Global Warming Skeptics," Press Release, U.S. Senate Committee on Environment and Public Works, October 11, 2006. For the original David Roberts blog, see Roberts, "The Denial Industry," Gristmill, September 19, 2006, http://grist mill.grist.org/print/2006/9/19/11408/1106?show_comments=no.

7. Brendan O'Neill, "Global Warming: The Chilling Effect on Free Speech," Spiked, October 6, 2006, www.spiked-online.com/index.php?/site/ article/1782/.

8. "Vast Majority of Evangelicals Not Represented by 'Evangelical Climate Initiative,'" ECI Fact Sheet, Interfaith Stewardship Alliance, 2006, http:// interfaithstewardship.org/pdf/ScientificOrthodoxiesPoliticizedScience.pdf.

9. Paul Watson, "The Beginning of the End for Life as We Know It on Planet Earth?" May 4, 2007,www.seashepherd.org/editorials/editorial_070504 _1.html.

10. "Evangelical Leaders Exploited by Global Warming—Population Control Lobby."

11. "Evangelical Leaders Exploited by Global Warming—Population Control Lobby."

12. "Evangelical Leaders Exploited by Global Warming—Population Control Lobby."

13. The initial number of signatories in February 2006 was eighty-six. By the time this article was published in September 2006, the number had increased.

14. Sheryl Henderson Blunt, "New Christian Coalition Says Fighting Global Warming Will Hurt the Poor," September 26, 2006, www.christianity today.com/ct/2006/010/8.26.html.

15. Blunt, "New Christian Coalition Says Fighting Global Warming Will Hurt the Poor."

16. Blunt, "New Christian Coalition Says Fighting Global Warming Will Hurt the Poor."

17. "Vast Majority of Evangelicals Not Represented by 'Evangelical Climate Initiative,' ECI Fact Sheet, Interfaith Stewardship Alliance, 2006, www.interfaithstewardship.org.

Chapter 11: Immigration and Racial Prejudice

1. Joseph Farah, "Illegal Aliens Murder 12 Americans Daily," WorldNetDaily.com, November 28, 2006, http://wnd.com/news/article.asp?ARTICLE_ID=53103.

2. All the information from Gary Cass in this chapter comes from "Reclaiming America for Christ" (Sunday school class, Coral Ridge Presbyterian Church, Ft. Lauderdale, FL, January 2006).

3. Nick Spencer, "The Far of Immigration," Connecting with Culture, December 17, 2004, http:// licc.org.uk/culture/fear-of-immigration.

4. Thomas Wenski, "What the Church Teaches About Immigration," *Our Sunday Visitor*, Huntington, IN, brochure.

5. "Immigration Debacle," *Washington Times*, May 21, 2007, 36, www.washingtontimes.com/op-ed/20070520–094056–4013r.htm.

6. David Limbaugh, "It's Not About Ethnicity; It's About the Law," *Washington Times*, May 28, 2007, 30.

Chapter 12: Marriage: Society's Smallest Unit

1. Tamar Lewin, "Alternative Marriages Likely to Jump in U.S.," *New York Times*, November 23, 2003, http://findarticles.com/p/articles/ mi_qn4188/is_20031123/ai_n11427113.

2. James Dobson, *Family News from Dr. James Dobson* (Colorado Springs, CO: Focus on the Family, September 2003), 4.

3. Linda J. Waite and Maggie Gallagher, *The Case for Marriage: Why Married People Are Happier, Healthier, and Better Off Financially* (New York: Doubleday, 2000), 186.

4. Barbara Dafoe Whitehead, *The Divorce Culture* (New York: Knopf, 1997), 188–89.

5. Charles Colson with Nancy R. Pearcey, *A Dangerous Grace: Daily Readings* (Dallas: Word, 1994), 189.

6. Betty Friedan, *The Feminine Mystique* (New York: Dell, 1963), 294.

7. Note that Christian scholars do not believe the death penalty is to be applied today for homosexuality or for many of the offenses listed in the Old Testament, with the exception of murder (see Genesis 9:6). There are three types of law in the Old Testament. First, there was *civil law.* These were the laws for the nation of Israel, which was a theocracy ruled by God, who was the only lawgiver in Zion. There was no parliament or congress in Israel to pass laws; God gave them all the laws they had. Those laws (the civil laws) have disappeared with the passing of the theocratic state of Judea in AD 70. You can detect the civil laws by the fact that they include temporal penalties, such as fines or whippings or death. Second, there were *ceremonial laws,* which prefigured and foreshadowed the coming of Jesus Christ as the Messiah. These were in the shadows, and when Christ appeared, the shadows fell away; so those ceremonial laws are now gone. The sin offering and the trespass offering and all such ceremonial laws pointed toward a religious object: the coming of the Messiah. But there remains the third part of God's law given at Sinai: the *moral law,* which is eternal and immutable, a reflection of the eternal and holy nature of God. This moral law is the very law of the living God for His moral creatures and can best be summed up in the Ten Commandments.

8. "Overall, 45 states have taken some form of legislative action to prohibit same-sex marriage; 26 of those states have voted to amend their state constitutions. The vast majority of those measures, though ratified by public referenda, originated in state legislatures" (Kerry Eleveld, "There Is a Gay Agenda—Winning Elections: Gay Millionaires and Their Allies Poured Unprecedented Sums into

the 2006 Election—and It Worked," Salon.com, November 29, 2006, www.salon.com/news/feature/2006/11/29/gay_millionaires/index.html.

9. Laurie Hall, *An Affair of the Mind: One Woman's Courageous Battle to Salvage Her Family from the Devastation of Pornography* (Colorado Springs: Focus on the Family, 1996), 11.

Chapter 13: Judicial Activism and the Courts

1. For more information, see David Gibbs II and Jerry Newcombe, *One Nation Under God: Ten Things Every Christian Should Know About the Founding of America* (Seminole, FL: Christian Law Association, 2003); John Eidsmoe, *Christianity and the Constitution: The Faith of Our Founding Fathers* (Grand Rapids: Baker, 1987); and David Barton, *Original Intent* (Aledo, TX: WallBuilder Press, 1996).

2. Henry Hyde, quoted in D. James Kennedy, *The Constitution in Crisis*, video (Fort Lauderdale, FL: Coral Ridge Ministries, September 20, 1987).

3. Thomas Jefferson, September 6, 1819, in Merrill D. Peterson, ed., *Jefferson Writings* (New York: Literary Classics of the United States, 1984), 1426.

4. Kermit L. Hall, ed., *The Oxford Companion to the Supreme Court of the United States* (New York: Oxford University Press, 1992), 79.

5. Robert Bork, quoted in D. James Kennedy, *We the People: Overruled*, video (Fort Lauderdale, FL: Coral Ridge Ministries, 2005).

6. David Limbaugh in Kennedy, *We the People*.

7. Robert Knight in Kennedy, *We the People*.

8. Gary Bauer in Kennedy, *We the People*.

9. Thomas Jefferson to Charles Hammond, in Saul K. Padover, ed., *Thomas Jefferson on Democracy* (New York: Appleton-Century, 1939), 64.

10. Thomas Jefferson to William Jarvis, September 28, 1820, in Wilson Whitman, ed., *Jefferson's Letters* (Eau Claire, WI: Hale & Co., 1900), 338.

11. Bork in Kennedy, *We the People*.

12. Abraham Lincoln, "First Inaugural Address," March 4, 1861, in *The Annals of America*, vol. 9, *1858–1865: The Crisis of the Union* (Chicago: Encyclopaedia Britannica, 1976), 254.

13. Wesley J. Smith in *We the People*.

14. Mat Staver in *We the People*.
15. Alexander Hamilton, James Madison, and John Jay, *The Federalist Papers* (New York: New American Library, 1961), 466.
16. Baron Charles Louis Montesquieu, *Spirit of Laws*, 1:186, quoted in Hamilton, Madison, and Jay, *The Federalist Papers*, footnote on 466.
17. Edwin Meese, in Kennedy, *We the People*.
18. Clarence Thomas, in Kennedy, *We the People*.
19. Gary Bauer, in Kennedy, *We the People*.

Chapter 14: The Problem of Political Compromise

1. Tony Perkins, "The Real San Fran Nancy," National Review, November 13, 2006, http://article.nationalreview.com/?q=MjhkOTdjYzIxYzViYmEx ZWM0YzAwOTM2ZDYyMDQ5YTQ=.
2. John Adams, quoted in Bill Federer, ed., *America's God and Country: Encyclopedia of Quotations* (St. Louis: Amerisearch, 2000), 10–11.
3. Blogs for Bush, www.blogsforbush.com/mt/arachives/007069.html.

Chapter 15: Put Not Your Trust in Princes

1. D. James Kennedy, *Can Reagan Save America?* (Fort Lauderdale: Coral Ridge Ministries, January 25, 1981).
2. Kennedy, *Can Reagan Save America?*
3. Kennedy, *Can Reagan Save America?*
4. Kennedy, *Can Reagan Save America?*
5. Interview with David Barton, Coral Ridge Ministries-TV, October 2002.
6. Jonathan Trumbull to George Washington, July 13, 1775, in Verna M. Hall and Rosalie J. Slater, *The Christian History of the American Revolution* (San Francisco: Foundation for American Christian Education, 1976), 511.
7. John Hancock, "A Proclamation for a Day of Public Thanksgiving," October 5, 1791, www.wallbuilders.org.
8. Daniel Lapin, "A Rabbi's Warning to U.S. Christians," WorldNetDaily, January 13, 2007, www.worldnetdaily.com/news/article.asp?ARTICLE _ID=53748.
9. Abraham Lincoln, quoted in J. B. McClure, ed., *Abraham Lincoln's Stories and Speeches* (Chicago: Rhodes & McClure, 1896), 185–86.

Epilogue: Something More Basic Than Politics

1. Jerry Newcombe also recommends a book that has helped him, a three-year through-the-Bible study guide: Alan Stibbed, ed., *Search the Scriptures* (Downers Grove, IL: IVP, 1949, 1974).
2. If you are in the continental United States, the staff at Coral Ridge Ministries can assist you in finding a church in your area. Write us with the appropriate details at Coral Ridge Ministries, Box 40, Fort Lauderdale, FL 33302.
3. You can request a copy of *Beginning Again* by writing to Coral Ridge Ministries, Box 40, Fort Lauderdale, FL 33302.

Appendix: Defending Religious Liberty

1. "Silent Night Secularized," WorldNetDaily.com, December 7, 2005, www.worldnetdaily.com/news/article.asp?ARTICLE_ID=47784.
2. While Thomas Jefferson may not have been fully orthodox in his beliefs as a professing Christian, he was far from the atheist some modern writers make him out to be. He was not anti-Christian in how he governed as president. Mark A. Beliles has assembled an impressive list of areas Jefferson supported the government being involved in:
    - ★ legislative and military chaplains
    - ★ establishing a national seal using a biblical symbol
    - ★ including the word *God* in our national motto
    - ★ official days of fasting and prayer on the state level
    - ★ punishing Sabbath breakers
    - ★ punishing marriages contrary to biblical law
    - ★ punishing irreverent soldiers
    - ★ protecting the property of churches
    - ★ requiring oaths use the words "so help me God" and be sworn on the Bible
    - ★ granting land to Christian schools
    - ★ allowing government property and facilities to be used for worship
    - ★ using the Bible and nondenominational religious instruction in the public schools (he was involved in three school districts, and the plan in each *required* that the Bible be taught in the public schools)

★ allowing clergymen to hold public office and encouraged them to do so

★ funding religious books for public libraries

★ funding salaries for missionaries

★ funding the construction of church buildings for Indians

★ exempting churches from taxation

★ establishing professional schools of theology (he wanted to bring the entire faculty of Calvin's seminary over from Geneva, Switzerland, and establish them at the University of Virginia)

★ writing treaties requiring other nations to guarantee religious freedom, including religious speeches and prayers in official ceremonies

These are not the actions of a man who was totally godless (see Mark A. Beliles's introduction to an updated version of *Thomas Jefferson's Abridgement of the Words of Jesus of Nazareth* [Charlottesville, VA: Providence Foundation, 1993], 11). For more information, see chapter 4, "The Real Thomas Jefferson," in D. James Kennedy and Jerry Newcombe, *What If America Were a Christian Nation Again?* (Nashville: Thomas Nelson, 2003).

3. Thomas Jefferson, "Virginia Bill for Establishing Religious Freedom," 1786, in Bruce Frohnen, ed., *The American Republic: Primary Sources* (Indianapolis: Liberty Fund, 2002), 330.

4. Bill Federer in D. James Kennedy, *One Nation Under God*, video (Fort Lauderdale, FL: Coral Ridge Ministries, 2005).

5. David C. Gibbs Jr. with Jerry Newcombe, *One Nation Under God: Ten Things Every Christian Should Know About the Founding of America* (Seminole, FL: Christian Law Association, 2003), 6–9.

6. "Men Jailed for Being on *Public Sidewalk*," WorldNetDaily.com, February 8, 2007, www.worldnetdaily.com/news/article.asp?ARTICLE_ID=54150.

7. Quoted in William A. Donohue, *Twilight of Liberty: The Legacy of the ACLU* (New Brunswick, NJ: Transaction Publishers, 1994), 6.

8. William Donohue, interview by Jerry Newcombe, Coral Ridge Ministries, January 8, 1991.

9. Donohue, *Twilight of Liberty*, 7.

10. Herb Titus, interview by Jerry Newcombe, Coral Ridge Ministries-TV, January 19, 2005.

11. Daniel Lapin, interview by Jerry Newcombe, Coral Ridge Ministries-TV, February 21, 2005.

12. Alan Sears, interview by Jerry Newcombe, Coral Ridge Ministries-TV, February 18, 2005.

13. See Donohue, *Twilight of Liberty,* 207–10.

14. Burt Neuborne, quoted in Donohue, *Twilight of Liberty,* 321.

15. Peter Lillback with Jerry Newcombe, *George Washington's Sacred Fire* (Bryn Mawr, PA: Providence Forum, 2006), 369.

16. Dwight D. Eisenhower, recorded for the "Back-to-God" program of the American Legion, February 20, 1955, quoted in William J. Federer, "Public Papers of Dwight D. Eisenhower 1953–1961," United States Folder in *Library of Classics* (St. Louis: AmeriSearch, Inc., 2002), CD-ROM.

17. First Charter of Virginia, in *The Annals of America,* vol. 1, *1493–1754: Discovering a New World* (Chicago: Encyclopaedia Britannica, 1976), 16.

18. The Mayflower Compact, in Bruce Frohnen, ed., *The American Republic: Primary Sources* (Indianapolis: Liberty Fund, 2002), 11.

19. William Bradford, in Samuel Eliot Morison, ed., *Of Plymouth Plantation, 1620–1647* (New York: Knopf, 2001), 61.

20. Fundamental Orders of Connecticut, January 14, 1639, quoted in Henry Steel Commager, ed., *Documents of American History,* 6th ed. (New York: Appleton-Century-Crofts, 1958), 26.

21. "The New England Confederation," in *1493–1754: Discovering a New World,* 172.

22. "The Declaration of Independence," in *The Annals of America,* vol. 2, *1755–1783: Resistance and Revolution* (Chicago: Encyclopaedia Britannica, 1976), 447.

23. Lillback with Newcombe, *George Washington's Sacred Fire.*

24. Quoted in Lillback with Newcombe, *George Washington's Sacred Fire,* 616–17.

25. George Washington, "Speech to the Delaware Chiefs," May 12, 1779, quoted in John Rhodehamel, comp., *George Washington: Writings* (New York: Literary Classics of the United States, 1997), 351.

26. These were the very men who wrote and adopted the Bill of Rights, the first ten amendments to the Constitution. The first of these amendments

contains the words against "an establishment of religion" that judges distort today as meaning there should be no public acknowledgment of God.

27. George Washington, "Proclamation of a National Day of Thanksgiving," October 3, 1789, in Jared Sparks, ed., *The Writings of George Washington,* 12 vols. (Boston: American Stationer's Company, 1837), 12:119.

28. Week after week, Washington attended churches with the Ten Commandments posted on the wall (as well as the Apostles' Creed and the Lord's Prayer). Examples of such churches are Pohick Church in Lorton, Virginia (the church he attended as a young adult), Christ Church in Philadelphia (where he attended while presiding over the Constitutional Convention in 1787), and Christ Church in Alexandria, Virginia (where he attended regularly after his presidency).

29. Quoted in Charles E. Rice, *The Supreme Court and Public Prayer: The Need for Restraint* (New York: Fordham University Press, 1964), 173.

30. Quoted in Rice, *Supreme Court and Public Prayer,* 175.

31. Quoted in Rice, *Supreme Court and Public Prayer,* 173.

32. Daniel Webster, quoted in "Building the Capitol," *Ten Years in Washington,* The Capital and the Bay, Library of Congress, http://memory.loc.gov/cgi-bin/query/r?ammem/lhbcb:@field(DOCID+@lit(lhbcb28043div15)).

33. The Court and Its Procedures, U.S. Supreme Court, www.supreme courtus.gov/about/procedures.pdf.

34. Building the White House, White House Historical Association, www.whitehousehistory.org/04/subs/04_a02_c.html.

35. William J. Federer, *America's God and Country: Encyclopedia of Quotations* (St. Louis: Amerisearch, 2000), 665–66.

36. Federer, *America's God and Country,* 665.

37. On These Walls, Library of Congress, www.loc.gov/loc/walls/jeff1.html.

38. On These Walls, Library of Congress, www.loc.gov/loc/walls/jeff2.html.

39. On These Walls, Library of Congress, www.loc.gov/loc/walls/jeff1.html.

40. On These Walls, Library of Congress, www.loc.gov/loc/walls/jeff1.html.

41. On These Walls, Library of Congress, www.loc.gov/loc/walls/jeff2.html.

42. Abraham Lincoln, "The Gettysburg Address," in *The Annals of America,* vol. 9, *1858–1865: The Crisis of the Union* (Chicago: Encyclopaedia Britannica, 1976), 463.

43. Quoted in *1858–1865: The Crisis of the Union,* 333.

44. Federer, *America's God and Country,* 351.

45. *Church of the Holy Trinity vs. United States,* 143 US 457, 36 L ed 226.

46. *Wallace v. Jaffree,* 472 U.S. 38 (1985), Justice William Rehnquist, dissenting, http://caselaw.lp.findlaw.com/scripts/getcase.pl?court=US&vol=472&invol=38.

47. Benjamin Hart, "The Wall That Protestantism Built: The Religious Reasons for the Separation of Church and State," *Policy Review,* Fall 1988, 44.

48. Richard N. Ostling, "In So Many Gods We Trust," *Time,* January 30, 1995, 72.

Index

About the Authors

D. JAMES KENNEDY, PhD, served as senior minister of Coral Ridge Presbyterian Church in Fort Lauderdale, Florida, for forty-eight years. He was the author of more than sixty-five books, including *New Every Morning, Why I Believe, Evangelism Explosion,* and *What If Jesus Had Never Been Born?* Kennedy earned a PhD in World Religion at New York University.

JERRY NEWCOMBE holds a bachelor's degree in history and a master's in communications. He is currently working on a doctorate at Knox Theological Seminary. Senior producer for Coral Ridge Ministries television and *The Coral Ridge Hour,* Newcombe has produced or coproduced more than fifty documentaries. The host of two weekly radio shows, he has also been a guest on numerous local and national television and radio talk shows and news programs. He and his wife live in Pompano Beach, Florida.